Junior High

CLAIM the Life

Semester 2

Journey

Development Team

Sarah Arthur, Durham, North Carolina
Janice Barrett, Avon, New York
John Jenkins, Ft. Worth, Texas
Ciona Rouse, Nashville, Tennessee
Will Penner, Consultant
Mark Thomas, Consultant
Jacquie Watlington, Consultant
John DeYoung, Video Producer
Josh Tinley, Associate Editor
Jenny Youngman, Development Editor
Crystal Zinkiewicz, Senior Editor

Editorial and Design Team

Crystal A. Zinkiewicz, Senior Editor
Keely Moore, Design Manager
Sheila K. Hewitt, Senior Production Editor
Susan Heinemann, Production Editor
Pam Shepherd, Production Editor

07 08 09 10 11 12 13 14 15 16—10 9 8 7 6 5 4 3 2 1

Cover Design: Keely Moore

Contents

Sessions

Session Guides . . .

CLAIM THE LIFE
Leader's Guide

<u>Today's Word</u>
Know where to focus.
Teach the language of the faith.

<u>Take-Away Learning and Scripture</u>
Give students a clear message from the Bible.

<u>Leader Information</u>
See the connections for yourself.

CD-ROM (included)
Access additional background, optional activities, music suggestions, and handouts.

The Session Plan

Tending
Help youth learn to
• Tend to God in their lives
• Tend to one another as a Christian community

Teaching
Two complete plans:
• Option A
"One Big Thing"—
More activity based
• Option B
"Q & D"—
More discussion oriented
Your choice!

Sending
• Youth identify their own learnings.
• Youth set their SMART goals as disciples of Christ.
• Send students forth with a blessing.

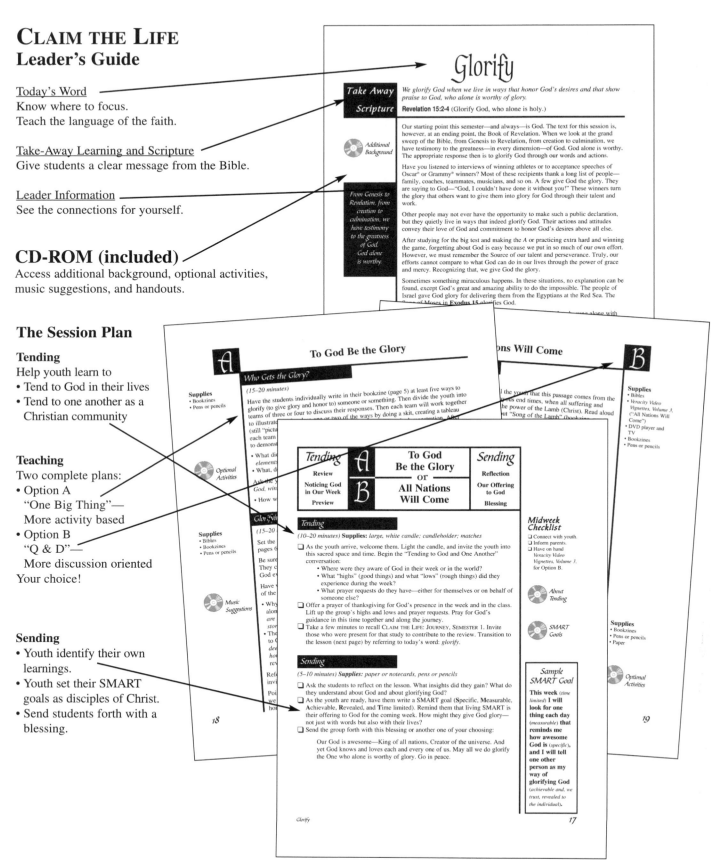

Glorify

We glorify God when we live in ways that honor God's desires and that show praise to God, who alone is worthy of glory.

Revelation 15:2-4 (Glorify God, who alone is holy.)

Additional Background

Our starting point this semester—and always—is God. The text for this session is, however, at an ending point, the Book of Revelation. When we look at the grand sweep of the Bible, from Genesis to Revelation, from creation to culmination, we have testimony to the greatness—in every dimension—of God. God alone is worthy. The appropriate response then is to glorify God through our words and actions.

Have you listened to interviews of winning athletes or to acceptance speeches of Oscar® or Grammy® winners? Most of these recipients thank a long list of people—family, coaches, teammates, musicians, and so on. A few give God the glory. They are saying to God—"God, I couldn't have done it without you!" These winners turn the glory that others want to give them into glory for God through their talent and work.

Other people may not ever have the opportunity to make such a public declaration, but they quietly live in ways that indeed glorify God. Their actions and attitudes convey their love of God and commitment to honor God's desires above all else.

After studying for the big test and making the *A* or practicing extra hard and winning the game, forgetting about God is easy because we put in so much of our own effort. However, we must remember the Source of our talent and perseverance. Truly, our efforts cannot compare to what God can do in our lives through the power of grace and mercy. Recognizing that, we give God the glory.

Sometimes something miraculous happens. In these situations, no explanation can be found, except God's great and amazing ability to do the impossible. The people of Israel gave God glory for delivering them from the Egyptians at the Red Sea. The Song of Moses in **Exodus 15** glorifies God.

From Genesis to Revelation, from creation to culmination, we have testimony to the greatness of God. God alone is worthy.

To God Be the Glory

Who Gets the Glory?

(15–20 minutes)

Have the students individually write in their bookzine (page 5) at least five ways to glorify (to give glory and honor to) someone or something. Then divide the youth into teams of three or four to discuss their responses. Then each team will work together to illustrate one or two of the ways by doing a skit, creating a tableau (still "picture . . .

• What di . . .
elements . . .
• What, d . . .

Ask the y . . .
God, win . . .
• How w . . .

Glorifying . . .

(15–20 . . .

Set the p . . .
pages 6 . . .

Be sure . . .
They c . . .
God ev . . .

Have . . .
of the . . .

• Why . . .
alon . . .
are . . .
stor . . .
• The . . .
to C . . .
dee . . .
ho . . .
rev . . .

Ref . . .
invi . . .

Poi . . .
we . . .
ho . . .

Supplies
• Bookzines
• Pens or pencils

Optional Activities

Supplies
• Bibles
• Bookzines
• Pens or pencils

Music Suggestions

18

All Nations Will Come

. . . l the youth that this passage comes from the
. . . ous end times, when all suffering and
. . . he power of the Lamb (Christ). Read aloud
. . . ut "Song of the Lamb" (bookzine . . .

Supplies
• Bibles
• *Veracity Video Vignettes, Volume 3,* ("All Nations Will Come")
• DVD player and TV
• Bookzines
• Pens or pencils

Tending	**A** **B**	**To God Be the Glory** or **All Nations Will Come**	*Sending*
Review Noticing God in Our Week Preview			Reflection Our Offering to God Blessing

Tending

(10–20 minutes) **Supplies:** *large, white candle; candleholder; matches*

☐ As the youth arrive, welcome them. Light the candle, and invite the youth into this sacred space and time. Begin the "Tending to God and One Another" conversation:
   • Where were they aware of God in their week or in the world?
   • What "highs" (good things) and what "lows" (rough things) did they experience during the week?
   • What prayer requests do they have—either for themselves or on behalf of someone else?
☐ Offer a prayer of thanksgiving for God's presence in the week and in the class. Lift up the group's highs and lows and prayer requests. Pray for God's guidance in this time together and along the journey.
☐ Take a few minutes to recall CLAIM THE LIFE: JOURNEY, SEMESTER 1. Invite those who were present for that study to contribute to the review. Transition to the lesson (next page) by referring to today's word: *glorify.*

Sending

(5–10 minutes) **Supplies:** *paper or notecards, pens or pencils*

☐ Ask the students to reflect on the lesson. What insights did they gain? What do they understand about God and about glorifying God?
☐ As the youth are ready, have them write a SMART goal (Specific, Measurable, Achievable, Revealed, and Time limited). Remind them that living SMART is their offering to God for the coming week. How might they give God glory—not just with words but also with their lives?
☐ Send the group forth with this blessing or another one of your choosing:

> Our God is awesome—King of all nations, Creator of the universe. And yet God knows and loves each and every one of us. May all we do glorify the One who alone is worthy of glory. Go in peace.

Midweek Checklist
☐ Connect with youth.
☐ Inform parents.
☐ Have on hand *Veracity Video Vignettes, Volume 3,* for Option B.

About Tending

SMART Goals

Sample SMART Goal

This week *(time limited)* **I will look for one thing each day** *(measurable)* **that reminds me how awesome God is** *(specific),* **and I will tell one other person as my way of glorifying God** *(achievable and, we trust, revealed to the individual).*

Supplies
• Bookzines
• Pens or pencils
• Paper

Optional Activities

19

Glorify

17

And More

Midweek Connections

Send midweek e-mails to youth and to parents. Personalize the e-mails if you wish. Or just hit SEND.

For the Students—Continue reaching students through the week.

For the Parents—Give the parents information so that they can engage their teens too.

Authorized Access to Additional Materials on *claimthelife.com*

Access information and links related to youth, teaching and learning, CLAIM THE LIFE, and much more!

- Administrative tools to make Midweek Connections simple
- Interactive versions of the Learning Plan and sample pages
- Helps for various groupings (all youth in one class, ninth graders with older youth, for example)
- Connections to church tradition

- Previews of the related Veracity Video Vignettes
- More about spiritual formation, practices of the faith, and ritual
- More about discipleship and accountability
- More about fostering Christian community
- Safe Sanctuary practices

- Asset development
- More about adolescent development and relating to teenagers
- Glossary of the words and definitions
- Ways to get more help (real people you can talk to)
- Certificates of completion

Additional Resources

ISBN-13: 9780687641741

Student Bookzine (one for each student)

Filled with crucial information—like a book
Colorful, with brief readings—like a magazine

To be used in class
To be sent home at the end of the study

Veracity Video Vignettes DVD (optional)

Five of the 16 Q & D (Option B) plans incorporate original 4- to 8-minute videos as discussion starters. Preview them online at *www.claimthelife.com*.

ISBN-13: 9780687643677

Themes in the CLAIM THE LIFE Series
Younger Youth

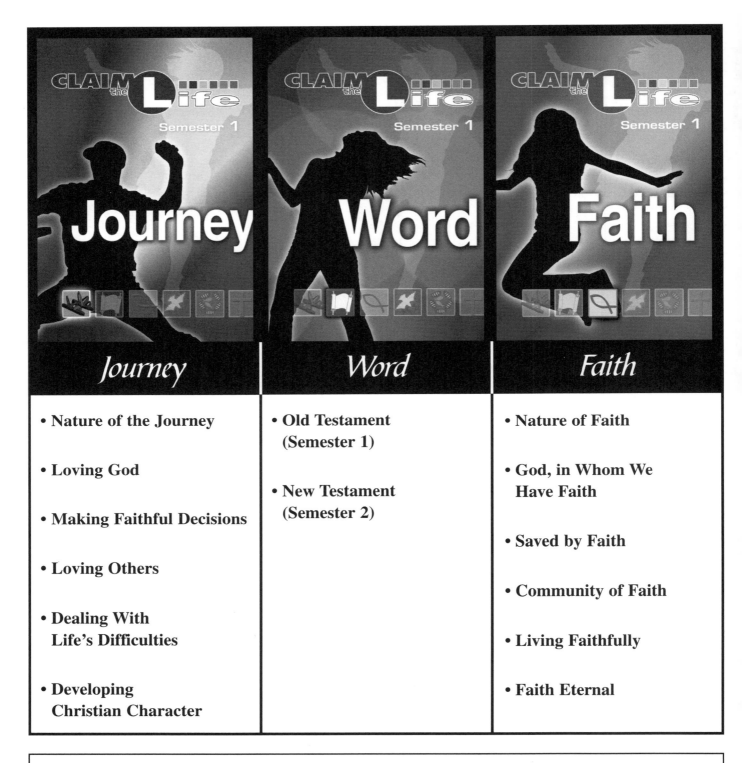

Journey	Word	Faith
• Nature of the Journey	• Old Testament (Semester 1)	• Nature of Faith
• Loving God	• New Testament (Semester 2)	• God, in Whom We Have Faith
• Making Faithful Decisions		• Saved by Faith
• Loving Others		• Community of Faith
• Dealing With Life's Difficulties		• Living Faithfully
• Developing Christian Character		• Faith Eternal

Visit *www.claimthelife.com* for the interactive Learning Plan.

What's Coming Next?
CLAIM THE LIFE: WORD

Some of our youth have played the great simulation game "Romans and Christians." In it "Roman soldiers" persecute the "early Christians," driving them into hiding. The faithful have no Bibles, no hymn books; they have only what they have committed to memory as they worship in the "catacombs." For the teens the game brings home the point that for many people throughout the centuries, to claim the life of Christian was not an easy thing. Being persecuted, even killed for one's beliefs, was not a game but a day-to-day reality.

What about today? We may joke about being stranded on a desert island, but we also know stories of prisoners of war and others who have had to rely on only the Scripture and hymns they had committed to memory to help sustain them. Less dramatic, but more common, all of us have or will go through times when, even if we have easy access to Bibles, having the words of Scripture come back to us in our minds provides comfort, clarity, or direction when we need it most.

CLAIM THE LIFE: WORD, the next study in this series, takes seriously the opportunity to help youth write on their heart the words of key Scriptures. The first semester pulls from the Old Testament; and the second, from the New Testament. Each lesson not only helps youth understand and claim the meaning of the text, but also helps them commit to memory the words, as well as the meaning.

Be sure to look at the Learning Plan on *www.claimthelife.com* for the specific passages. These were chosen especially because of their power to guide, comfort, and shape the lives and faith of the youth.

Also Coming: *Veracity Video Vignettes, Volumes 5 and 6*

As with CLAIM THE LIFE: JOURNEY, WORD will also have visual discussion starters as an option for teaching. Semester 1's videos (Volume 5) will relate to these words: *Sabbath, Honor, Majestic, Heart,* and *Justice.* Semester 2's (Volume 6) will relate to these words: *Riches, Offering, Good Shepherd, Youth,* and *Support.*

**Thy word is a lamp to my feet
and a light unto my path.**
(Psalm 119:105)

Visit *www.claimthelife.com* for the Scriptures used.

An Overview of CLAIM THE LIFE: JOURNEY

Semester 1

Theme	Key Word	Reference	Annotation
Nature of the Journey	Journey	Hebrews 12:1-2	Let us run the race before us.
Loving God	Worship	John 4:23-24	Worship in spirit and truth
	Praying	Matthew 7:7-12	Ask; search; knock.
Making Faithful Decisions	Image of God	Genesis 1:26-31	God makes humankind in God's own image.
	Commitment	Daniel 3:17-18	The faithful face the fiery furnace.
	Follow	Luke 9:23-25	Take up your cross and follow me.
	Temple	1 Corinthians 6:19-20	Your body is the temple of the Holy Spirit.
Loving Others	Forgiving	Matthew 18:21-22	Forgive seventy-seven times.
	Kindness	Ephesians 4:25–5:2	Be kind to one another; live in love.
	Servant	John 13:1-17	Jesus washes the disciples' feet.
Dealing With Life's Difficulties	Suffering	Romans 5:1-5	We boast in our suffering.
	Endurance	James 5:7-11	Be patient and endure in suffering.
Developing Christian Character	Purity	1 John 3:1-3	Purify yourself as Christ is pure.
	Courage	Joshua 1:6-9	Be strong and courageous.
	Simplicity	Luke 12:22-31	Consider the lilies of the field.
	Goodness	Titus 3:4-8	Devote yourself to good works.

This Semester (2)

Theme	Key Word	Reference	Annotation
Loving God	Glorify	Revelation 15:2-4	Glorify God, who alone is holy.
	Devotion	1 Kings 8:54-61	Devote yourself completely to God.
	Beloved	1 John 4:7-12	Beloved, love on another; love is from God.
Making Faithful Decisions	Decision	Luke 5:1-11	The fishermen decide to follow Jesus.
	Disciple	Luke 14:25-33	Discipleship has a cost.
	Abstain	Galatians 5:16-21	Live by the Spirit.
Loving Others	Love	Galatians 5:13-15	The whole law summed up: "Love your neighbor."
	Action	1 John 3:16-18	Let us love in truth and action.
	Honesty	Deuteronomy 25:13-19	All who act dishonestly God abhors.
	Hospitality	Hebrews 13:1-2	Do not neglect hospitality.
Dealing With Life's Difficulties	Brokenness	Psalm 51:16-17	I can come to God with my brokenness.
	Hardship	Genesis 41:46-52	God has made me forget all my hardship.
Developing Christian Character	Generosity	Deuteronomy 15:7-11	Open your hand to the poor and needy.
	Fruitful	John 15:1-5	Apart from me you cannot bear fruit.
	Humility	Luke 14:7-11	In humility choose the lowest place.
	Light	Matthew 5:14-16	You are the light of the world.

The Learning Plan: Faith Knowledge

Two questions regularly surface around youth Sunday school: What should our youth know? and Why do we keep losing our older youth? The questions are connected.

Too many youth Sunday school opportunities are wasted because churches have no plan for what youth should know. Often congregations are so relieved to have someone—anyone—take the youth class that "whatever you want to do" is all right with them. When the older youth begin to drift away, the assumptions are that they are too busy or that Sunday school just isn't fun enough. In reality, teens may feel that "nothing's happening, so why bother to going?" Of course, something's happening; but it may not be meaningful enough for youth to make attendance a priority. Meeting that challenge requires a good plan, good resources, and good teaching.

Consider how we learn: Something piques our interest; we gather information from multiple sources (a documentary, an article, or a talk with an expert or a fan); we try out what we know so far, connecting our experience to the information and vocabulary we have been learning. Then we build on that knowledge again: Our interest grows; we search for more information; we try out what we know, connecting our growing information and vocabulary to our experiences. And so the cycle continues. Interest leads to knowledge; knowledge leads to greater interest. However, if we have no information or vocabulary, we are not be able to make connections and name our experiences. The growth stops; the interest lies unfulfilled.

Interest leads to knowledge; knowledge leads to greater interest.

Apply those principles to faith. Having a faith vocabulary and information gives us knowledge to name our experiences; we are able to make connections with faith that make life meaningful. A key to increasing faith is a plan to increase faith knowledge.

The Learning Plan (pages 6–8) **for CLAIM THE LIFE is well thought out,** building on major themes of the Christian faith: Journey, Word, Faith, Promise, Story, and Call. Within each theme, the six-year plan focuses on one word (or phrase) to give youth (and leaders) a strong vocabulary of faith. This way, the words they hear in church make sense to them. Both semesters of a theme have the same sub-themes; the key words are different, but the repetition of the sub-themes provides good educational reinforcement. Visit the Learning Plan on *claimthelife.com* for more details.

A key to increasing faith is a plan to increase faith knowledge.

CLAIM THE LIFE provides the intentionality that leaders seek when they think about not wasting the precious six years we have with youth. These teachers want to provide the basics of "what youth should know." This plan is also intentional about not planning everything. Each congregation, each class, each teacher, each youth is unique. So CLAIM THE LIFE does not fill every week in the year but leaves room for serendipity, for local traditions, for variety—some spice to go with the main meal.

In educational circles, the term *rigor* is emerging as a way to describe a growing commitment to present students with more challenging course work. And students are rising to those higher standards and finding the challenge meaningful and fun. CLAIM THE LIFE offers the rigor of a satisfying, excellent course of learning

Tending: Spiritual Formation

Off the top of your head, name three spiritual practices.

You probably thought of prayer, Bible study, meditation, silence, or worship. But if you had exhausted your list of faith-forming practices, would you have included Sunday school among them?

The creators of CLAIM THE LIFE want to challenge you to dream about what your youth Sunday school program would look like if you approached that sometimes-chaotic hour on Sundays as a faith-forming experience—a spiritual practice for youth.

Thinking about Sunday school as a spiritual practice changes the way you approach it, plan it, and prepare for it. When you think about that hour on Sunday as sacred time when Christ is being formed in you and the youth, your dream of what God can do through you grows. "Christian practices," even Sunday school, "help us loosen our grip on the wrong things so that we can reach toward the right things. They till the soul-soil, knead the clay, and loosen our knotted lives a little" (*Soul Tending: Life-Forming Practices for Older Youth and Young Adults,* Abingdon Press, 2002; page 13).

CLAIM THE LIFE **offers you a chance to invite your youth** to the journey of faith, understanding that growth happens at every stop along the way. Sunday school is one of those grace-filled places on the road where youth learn to be community, grow together, grow closer to God, and learn what being a follower of Jesus means.

Weekdays for teenagers are filled with school, studies, practices, homework, hang-out time, work, and who knows what else. Imagine if Sunday school felt like a cup of grace and love for your worn-out teens.

In CLAIM THE LIFE, **each Sunday morning begins with a ritual** called Tending. Week after week, students are invited into sacred space, challenged to tend to God in their week and in their world. Initially students may be reticent to speak, but the ritual and weekly reminder help them learn to look for God in their lives. Soon they are more able to see the signs of God's presence and feel more confident to articulate them.

Tending to God naturally leads to tending to one another. Students hear the highs and lows, the joys and concerns of their class members, and learn to listen and to act (in other words, to tend to them). The group becomes the Christian community they are learning about.

At one time Readin', 'Ritin', and 'Rithmetic were considered the basics of education. But recent work in educational circles indicates a new way of thinking about what's truly basic in learning: Relationships, Rigor, and Relevance. CLAIM THE LIFE follows those principles and adds one: *Ritual*.

Taking time, week after week, for the Tending ritual develops closer relationships with one another and with God. In past Sunday school times, teachers felt compelled to quash the "chit chat" to get to the "real lesson"; but CLAIM THE LIFE recognizes the hunger for life-giving relationships. Tending is one way to feed your youth spiritually.

Thinking about Sunday school as a spiritual practice changes the way you approach it, plan it, and prepare for it.

Tending to God naturally leads to tending to one another.

Teaching: More Than One Way

One size does not fit all. Every class, every teacher, and every youth is different, even from day to day. So CLAIM THE LIFE gives you two ways to engage your students. Each option is a complete lesson plan in itself.

Option A is affectionately called "One Big Thing." Although the description isn't particularly creative, the lessons definitely are. The one big thing usually requires students to move, plan, and work together in some way. The majority of lesson time is spent with the youth doing something. Out of that task then comes the discussion, the connections to the Scripture, the aha moments.

Option B is called "Q & D." Playing off "Q & A," this option may seem more like traditional classroom question-and-answer teaching; but it has a twist. Rather than teaching for the "right answer," the questions in this option stimulate discussion and thinking. The creative lead-ins jump-start meaningful discussion and connections to the Scripture.

Each option is a complete lesson plan in itself.

Persons learn in various ways. Howard Gardner, noted author, psychologist, and professor of neuroscience at Harvard University, has identified at least seven ways, calling them "multiple intelligences." According to Gardner, the preferred way of learning for a student may be verbal, visual, interpersonal (within groups), intrapersonal (alone), logical, musical, or kinesthetic (movement). Persons usually have more than one intelligence that is relatively strong, but the other ones may be a struggle for them. Recognizing this situation, CLAIM THE LIFE teaching plans use a variety of the intelligences.

- **Tending** engages the group, uses candles, and encourages youth to talk. This ritual appeals to interpersonal, visual, and verbal intelligences.

- **Option A** uses interpersonal, logical, and kinesthetic learning styles more frequently than the other intelligences.

- **Option B** relies more on verbal, visual, and musical learning styles.

- **Sending** is intentional about giving youth time for personal reflection, which is intrapersonal intelligence.

Veracity Video Vignettes are an option within Option B. Five of the sixteen lessons have video discussion starters. These 4- to 8-minute original works may be in the style of a music video, a documentary, a series of interviews, a story, or a parody. Previews are on the website.

Veracity Video Vignettes Volume 3
- Glorify: "All Nations Will Come"
- Abstain: "So Cool?"
- Hospitality: "SWAT"
- Generosity: "Who Answered the Call?"
- Humility: "Altar Ego"

With CLAIM THE LIFE, you have the tools to best fit your class's distinct needs and interests. As you prepare, read through both options. Choose the one you feel is better suited to your group. If you find yourself using more of Option A, for example, be intentional about occasionally choosing Option B and vice versa. Or create your own from a combination or adaptation from both. Or do both!

You're in charge.

Sending: Discipleship

A disciple is a follower; surely discipleship is "follow-through." We can teach the greatest lessons; but without follow-through on the part of our students, our efforts have little impact. How do we help youth grow in their discipleship?

CLAIM THE LIFE sessions begin with Tending to God and to one another. Then the Teaching takes place—either Option A or B. But the learning and growing aren't complete without the Sending.

The Sending ritual has three elements:

> _Discipleship is "follow-through."_

- **Personal and group reflection.** "OK, we've finished the lesson; it's time to go to worship (or home, or wherever)! Sure hope you've 'got it.' " Rush, rush, rush! So much to do. No time to think.

  However, personal reflection time is crucial to learning. So built into the Sending ritual is a time for silence, when each youth can listen for the still, small voice of God.

  The reflection time does not have to be long—perhaps two or three minutes. That time may seem like forever at first; but as your group grows more comfortable with the silence, they will be better able to enter into that place where they can truly hear God's direction.

- **SMART goals.** A typical goal for a Sunday school lesson could be to "be kinder." That aim is nice, but it's about as effective as "Lose some weight." A SMART goal, on the other hand, for those of us who struggle with weight could be "Walk one mile a day, five days a week for one month." A "be kinder" SMART goal could be "Take my little sister to the park one day this week so that Mom can get a break."

> _Personal and group reflection and creating individual SMART goals are direct paths to relevance._

  SMART stands for **S**pecific, **M**easurable, **A**chievable, **R**evealed, and **T**ime limited. Businesses have been using variations of SMART goals for years to help employees and planners work more effectively. Various words fit the acronym, depending upon the purpose. The key variation that CLAIM THE LIFE uses is R for _revealed_. We want youth to learn to listen to what the Holy Spirit is revealing to them as individuals as they write their SMART goals. That spiritual discipline takes practice and comes out of the personal and group reflection time.

- **Blessing.** The Sending ritual ends with a benediction, a blessing for the group. These words remind the youth that God calls them forth into the world _and_ that God goes with them. The sacred space named in the beginning Tending ritual is not limited to the Sunday school room.

In educational circles, the new three _R_s are _relationships, rigor,_ and _relevance_. All three are crucial for learning. But _relevance_ may be the hardest. Because each person is unique, what is relevant for one may not have any relevance for another. We do our best in the class to "make the material relevant," but ultimately learners take in what fits their particular needs. Personal and group reflection and creating individual SMART goals are direct paths to relevance.

The Sending ritual helps youth learn how to follow through with what they have experienced and learned. They will grow in their discipleship.

Web: Midweek Connections and More

Your youth are in Sunday school only one hour a week. Who's teaching them the other 167 hours in the week? With faith as the bedrock of all else we do, why should teaching it rate so little time?

CLAIM THE LIFE can't solve that dilemma, but it can give you ways to connect with both your students and their parents midweek. When you access the website (*claimthelife.com*), you will be able to enter the e-mail addresses of your students and of their parents once and use the website to send messages to them each week.

CLAIM THE LIFE provides the content related to the lessons, but you can customize it. Select portions or all of it; change the wording to make it your own, or add more content, if you choose. Send your message to everyone on your list, or personalize your message for just a few. Either way, just hit send. As an alternative, you can choose to create and send a text message, or you might cut and paste and send a snail-mail note. The hard work is done for you. You can concentrate on building the relationships and teaching.

- **To Parents.** The Midweek Connections tell parents that important things are happening in youth Sunday school. They know the word, the Scripture, and the focus. The message gives parents something to talk about and something to do with their teen. In the Study of Effective Christian Education, Search Institute discovered that conversations about faith between parents and teens are formative for youth. The Midweek Connection you send is not just to parents; in effect, you give them the tools and opportunity to connect with their youth in a special, life-giving way.

- **To Youth.** Your Midweek Connections help you build relationships with your youth. Your message, both in content and in the very fact that you sent it, will be a factor in their continuing spiritual formation and discipleship.

The website, *www.claimthelife.com,* is also for you. It includes not only the helps on the CD-ROM, but also much more that is only for you as an authorized user:

- Administrative tools to make Midweek Connections simple
- Interactive versions of the Learning Plan and sample pages
- Helps for various groupings (youth in one class, ninth graders with older ones)
- Previews of the related Veracity Video Vignettes
- Connections to church tradition
- More about spiritual formation, practices of the faith, and ritual
- More about discipleship, accountability, and relevance
- More about fostering Christian community and relationships
- More about teaching and learning and rigor
- More about adolescent development and relating to teenagers
- Safe Sanctuary practices
- Asset development
- Additional links
- Suggestions for other studies
- Certificates of completion; other celebration ideas
- Ways to get more help (real people you can talk to)

The Midweek Connections tell parents—and youth—that important things are happening in youth Sunday school.

 *Web Access Information*

The website is an additional resource for you.

About Younger Youth

Here are some developmental characteristics of younger youth:

Physical	• Bodies rapidly changing • Wide variation of maturation within classroom
Sexuality	• Linked to own body • Curious about opposite sex
Parents	• Still linked to parents • Rebel in brief spurts
Peers	• Friends very important • Run in packs
Thinking	• Mostly concrete with occasions of abstract thinking • More likely to accept what they are taught • Heavily dependent upon direct experience • Limited attention span
Verbal Skills	• Slowly developing • Hesitant to practice skills, lest they appear stupid • Slowness to answer may be a weighing of options
Invincibility	• Bad things happen only to others • Behavior doesn't always reflect stated choices • Find it difficult to project too far into the future • Can't easily visualize consequences
Morals, Values	• Take on values of parents • Decisions are clear; no ambiguity • Follow group mentality for many decisions
Faith	• God: abstract but benevolent • Find God in church or youth group (affiliative) • Need stories of Jesus as concrete examples of faithful living

For more developmental characteristics of younger youth, visit the web exclusives section of *www.claimthelife.com*.

Meet the Writers

Marcey Balcomb wrote "Disciple" and "Light." A thirty-two-year veteran in youth ministry, Marcey cares deeply about guiding youth to intentionally shape their lives as disciples and live their faith every day. She is the author of the *Single-Digit Youth Groups* series and several other resources. She lives in Portland, Oregon.

Larry Beman, who wrote "Decision" and "Honesty," has worked extensively with youth over the years and has recently been enriched by work camp experiences with junior and senior highs. He lives near Rochester, New York.

Mary Bernard is a Christian educator with a masters degree in curriculum and instruction as well. She is also writing for the *Amazing Bible Race* website. Mary wrote "Generosity"; she lives in Nashville.

Anne Broyles wrote "Devotion" and "Love." An ordained clergyperson and seasoned curriculum writer, her current focus is writing books. Her newest, *Priscilla and the Hollyhocks* (2008), is the true story of a slave girl who walked the Trail of Tears. Anne lives on a New England lake where she kayaks among great blue herons.

Robin Kimbrough wrote "Glorify," "Action," and "Hardship." Previously the Assistant Attorney General for the State of Tennessee, she has seen the effects of not following Jesus. She is ordained and currently serving Scott United Methodist Church, outside Nashville.

John Losey wrote "Fruitful" and "Humility." He is the Director of Praxis Training Systems, consulting for churches, mission organizations, businesses, and universities. Along with speaking, writing, and facilitating and leading workshops, John also enjoys teaching Scuba diving, backpacking, and quiet water paddling. He lives in Lake Forest, California.

Barb McCreight wrote "Brokenness." She has seen her faith journey take her from public school teaching to youth ministry and continuing on toward deacons orders as a servant of God. She is currently serving as youth minister at First United Methodist Church in Bryant, Arkansas.

Mike Ratliff wrote "Abstain." A local church youth minister for more than thirty years, he is currently serving the global church as the Associate General Secretary of the Division on Ministry With Young People for The United Methodist Church. His most recent book, *Sacred Challenge,* focuses on re-inventing the Sunday school.

Janie Wilkerson works on the *Journal of Student Ministries* and has spent several years as a volunteer in youth ministry. With a daughter fast approaching teen age, she and her husband, David, are buckling in for the roller-coaster ride of adolescence in their own family. Janie wrote "Hospitality" and contributed to "Beloved," two areas of passion for her.

Crys Zinkiewicz also contributed to "Beloved." That word has become more and more important to her in her own faith journey. Crys is the senior editor for Abingdon Youth resources, including CLAIM THE LIFE.

To learn more about the writers, visit *www.claimthelife.com.*

Glorify

We glorify God when we live in ways that honor God's desires and that show praise to God, who alone is worthy of glory.

Revelation 15:2-4 (Glorify God, who alone is holy.)

 *Additional Background*

From Genesis to Revelation, from creation to culmination, we have testimony to the greatness of God. God alone is worthy.

Our starting point this semester—and always—is God. The text for this session is, however, at an ending point, the Book of Revelation. When we look at the grand sweep of the Bible, from Genesis to Revelation, from creation to culmination, we have testimony to the greatness—in every dimension—of God. God alone is worthy. The appropriate response then is to glorify God through our words and actions.

Have you listened to interviews of winning athletes or to acceptance speeches of Oscar® or Grammy® winners? Most of these recipients thank a long list of people—family, coaches, teammates, musicians, and so on. A few give God the glory. They are saying to God—"God, I couldn't have done it without you!" These winners turn the glory that others want to give them into glory for God through their talent and work.

Other people may not ever have the opportunity to make such a public declaration, but they quietly live in ways that indeed glorify God. Their actions and attitudes convey their love of God and commitment to honor God's desires above all else.

After studying for the big test and making the *A* or practicing extra hard and winning the game, forgetting about God is easy because we put in so much of our own effort. However, we must remember the Source of our talent and perseverance. Truly, our efforts cannot compare to what God can do in our lives through the power of grace and mercy. Recognizing that, we give God the glory.

Our efforts cannot compare to what God can do in our lives. Recognizing that, we give God the glory.

Sometimes something miraculous happens. In these situations, no explanation can be found, except God's great and amazing ability to do the impossible. The people of Israel gave God glory for delivering them from the Egyptians at the Red Sea. The Song of Moses in **Exodus 15** glorifies God.

In **Revelation 15:2-4** is another such song, the Song of the Lamb, sung along with the Song of Moses. Both recognize God's great and mighty deeds. The people standing before the throne of God (indicated by the reference to the "sea of glass") are victorious in the battle with the beast. They know that they have conquered not because of their own efforts but because of God's power and authority. They did not get to this point without great suffering for their faith. In fact, they had been killed.

The people beside the sea had kept their faith in the face of persecution by the Romans and were martyred for their choice. They may not have survived on earth, but they obtained the victory in heaven and now are in the presence of the Lord, glorifying God.

Can we still sing a song of praise and redemption when bad things happen? Can we give God glory when it would be easier to accept glory for ourselves? Can we live in ways that show our love for God and our desire to serve? Then we glorify God!

Tending	A̲̅ B̲̅	To God Be the Glory — or — All Nations Will Come	Sending
Review Noticing God in Our Week Preview			Reflection Our Offering to God Blessing

Tending

(10–20 minutes) **Supplies:** *large, white candle; candleholder; matches*

❏ As the youth arrive, welcome them. Light the candle, and invite the youth into this sacred space and time. Begin the "Tending to God and One Another" conversation:
  - Where were they aware of God in their week or in the world?
  - What "highs" (good things) and what "lows" (rough things) did they experience during the week?
  - What prayer requests do they have—either for themselves or on behalf of someone else?

❏ Offer a prayer of thanksgiving for God's presence in the week and in the class. Lift up the group's highs and lows and prayer requests. Pray for God's guidance in this time together and along the journey.

❏ Take a few minutes to recall CLAIM THE LIFE: JOURNEY, SEMESTER 1. Invite those who were present for that study to contribute to the review. Transition to the lesson (next page) by referring to today's word: *glorify*.

Sending

(5–10 minutes) **Supplies:** *paper or notecards, pens or pencils*

❏ Ask the students to reflect on the lesson. What insights did they gain? What do they understand about God and about glorifying God?

❏ As the youth are ready, have them write a SMART goal (**S**pecific, **M**easurable, **A**chievable, **R**evealed, and **T**ime limited). Remind them that living SMART is their offering to God for the coming week. How might they give God glory—not just with words but also with their lives?

❏ Send the group forth with this blessing or another one of your choosing:

> Our God is awesome—King of all nations, Creator of the universe. And yet God knows and loves each and every one of us. May all we do glorify the One who alone is worthy of glory. Go in peace.

Midweek Checklist
❏ Connect with youth.
❏ Inform parents.
❏ Have on hand *Veracity Video Vignettes, Volume 3,* for Option B.

 *About Tending*

 *SMART Goals*

Sample SMART Goal

This week (*time limited*) **I will look for one thing each day** (*measurable*) **that reminds me how awesome God is** (*specific*)**, and I will tell one other person as my way of glorifying God** (*achievable and, we trust, revealed to the individual*)**.**

To God Be the Glory

Supplies
• Bookzines
• Pens or pencils

Optional Activities

(15–20 minutes)

Have the students individually write in their bookzine (page 5) at least five ways to glorify (to give glory and honor to) someone or something. Then divide the youth into teams of three or four to discuss their responses. Then each team will work together to illustrate for the class one or two of the ways by doing a skit, creating a tableau (still "picture" of an action frozen in place), or doing a simple demonstration. After each team has presented its way(s), invite the team to talk about what ways they chose to demonstrate and why. When all of the groups have presented, ask:

• What did you see in common in these presentations? (*positive, upbeat, happy elements; the person or thing was worthy of the glory*)
• What, do you think, does it mean to glorify or give glory to someone or something?

Ask the youth to give some examples of whom or what people glorify (*for example, God, winners, physical beauty, having money, celebrities*). List their answers, then ask:

• How worthy do you think each of these is of our honor? Why? [Encourage debate.]

Glorifying God in Death and in Life

Supplies
• Bibles
• Bookzines
• Pens or pencils

Music Suggestions

(15–20 minutes)

Set the context for the Scripture. Direct the youth to do "Code Breaker" (bookzine, pages 6–7). (Answers: 1. B; 2. D; 3. F; 4. A; 5. E; 6. C)

Be sure that the youth understand that "those who had conquered" were actually killed. They conquered—not because they survived, but because they remained faithful to God even in the face of death. They are now singing in heaven, glorifying God.

Have volunteers read aloud **Revelation 15:2-4** from their Bibles or from pages 6 and 8 of the bookzine. Ask:

• Why, do you think, would the writer of Revelation include the "song of Moses" along with the "song of the Lamb"? What do these songs have in common? (*Both are songs of rejoicing for a miraculous deliverance—at the Red Sea and in the story depicted in Revelation.*)
• These people had suffered and died for their faith, and yet they were singing glory to God. Why? What were they saying about God? (*Great and amazing are your deeds; Just and true are your ways; For you alone are holy. God is worthy of such honor.*) [Remind the youth that *fear* in this context means to have awe and reverence for God.]

Refer the youth to "To God Be the Glory" (bookzine, page 9). After a few minutes, invite volunteers to give some of their thoughts.

Point out that people who are not believers look at how we live as to whom or what we glorify. Our actions speak loudly. As Christians, we are to love, worship, honor—that is, *glorify*—God, who alone is holy.

All Nations Will Come

Hallelujah, God Reigns!

(15–25 minutes)

Set the context for today's Scripture. Tell the youth that this passage comes from the Book of Revelation and talks about the joyous end times, when all suffering and wrong in the world will be overcome by the power of the Lamb (Christ). Read aloud **Revelation 15:2-4** from the Bible. Point out "Song of the Lamb" (bookzine, page 8), and introduce the video as a contemporary song that glorifies God.

Play the video. Ask:

• Given the Scripture and the video, what do you think the word *glorify* means?

Divide the youth into three teams. Tell them that you will replay the video and that this time they are to listen and watch for specific things. Refer them to "All Nations Will Come" (bookzine, page 10). Give each team one of the following instructions:

Team 1: Watch for, listen for, and take notes on images or key phrases that describe the extent of who is glorifying God. (*Africa, Amazon, Asia; all God's children; four winds [North, East, South, West]; towers of cathedrals to the faithful gathered underground [public and accepted to secret in the face of persecution]; dawn of creation; not just church bells, but all God's children*)

Team 2: Watch and listen for descriptions of the power of God (*powers of dark tremble; felled by a single Word [Christ] or word, love*)

Team 3: Look at who is included and where God is glorified. (*All races, nations, genders, ages; in major milestones like a wedding, in everyday times, as well as in church [baptism]*).

If you have time, play the video a third time. Give the teams time to report their findings to the class. (Suggestions are in italic above.) Talk about the implications of the information; see "Us Too!" (bookzine, page 10). (*God is worthy; one response is to glorify God.*)

Love Song

(10–15 minutes)

Refer the youth to the text of the "Song of the Lamb" (bookzine, page 8). Ask:

• What connections do you see in these ancient and contemporary songs? (*One connection is that they both glorify God, who is worthy of that honor.*)

Have the youth work in groups of two or three to quickly make a list of contemporary love songs and then write their own love song to glorify God. The tune may be original, or students may write new lyrics to an existing tune. Invite volunteers to perform their songs before the class.

Or simply replay the video and encourage everyone to sing along, at least with the chorus.

Supplies
• Bibles
• *Veracity Video Vignettes, Volume 3,* ("All Nations Will Come")
• DVD player and TV
• Bookzines
• Pens or pencils

Supplies
• Bookzines
• Pens or pencils
• Paper

Optional Activities

Devotion

Devotion to God is an attitude that pervades everything in our lives, especially our loyalties and priorities.

1 Kings 8:54-61 (Devote yourself completely to God.)

Additional Background

Solomon, the son of King David and Bathsheba, was the third king of Israel. His name is synonymous with wisdom and wealth. Part of the legacy of his 40-year reign was the Jerusalem Temple he had built over a seven-year period.

When the house of the Lord was finished, King Solomon dedicated the Temple for the name of the Lord (**1 Kings 8:22-53**) and blessed those assembled. Solomon gave glory to God, reminded his audience of how God had kept promises, and encouraged them to devote themselves "completely to the Lord our God," keeping the commandments and living as covenant people.

Dedication of the Temple was a natural stage in the faith journey of God's chosen people. God brought them out of slavery in Egypt, led them to the Promised Land, and helped them create a new life for themselves—all as part of the covenant God made with them: "I will be your God, and you shall be my people" (**Jeremiah 7:23**). The Israelites devoted their lives to God because God's actions had already proven God's love for them.

Devotion is a seldom-used word in our culture. Youth will articulate strong feelings of love and loyalty for their friends, their pets, their favorite rock group or movie star, without using the word. Perhaps they consider themselves "passionate about" recycling or an AIDS Walk or their school basketball team. But even for those teens who regularly attend church and Sunday school, devotion to God may be a new concept.

Devotion to God, or passionate faith, shows through our thoughts, feelings, and actions.

Devotion to God, or passionate faith, shows through our thoughts, feelings, and actions. Prayer and worship time are the most obvious times of devotion, but our love and loyalty for God become an attitude that pervades everything. In contemplating a particular action the believer might ask, How does my relationship with God influence how I act? In relating to other people, our devotion to—passion for—God affects and can transform how we see others and how they see us.

This week you will have the opportunity to help young believers choose to put their devotion to God first so that it pervades everything else in their lives. All of their other loyalties should spring from this primary devotion.

Helping youth on their spiritual journey reminds each of us how our own passion for God makes a difference in our life and world.

Such passionate faith bestows inner strength (God is always with me) and can be a touchstone for making decisions, relating to others, and prioritizing time and energy. As always, helping youth on their spiritual journey reminds each of us how our own passion for God makes a difference in our life and world.

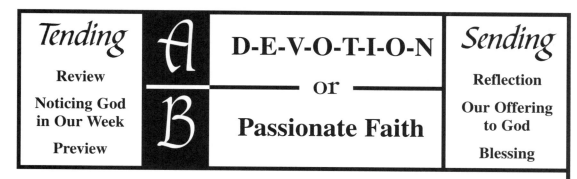

Tending	A B	D-E-V-O-T-I-O-N or Passionate Faith	Sending
Review Noticing God in Our Week Preview			Reflection Our Offering to God Blessing

Tending

(10–20 minutes) **Supplies:** *large, white candle; candleholder; matches*

❑ As the youth arrive, welcome them. Light the candle, and invite the youth into this sacred space and time. Begin the "Tending to God and One Another" conversation:
  - Where were they aware of God in their week or in the world?
  - What "highs" (good things) and what "lows" (rough things) did they experience during the week?
  - What prayer requests do they have—either for themselves or on behalf of someone else?

❑ Ask the youth about their SMART goal. If they tried to live out their "offering to God" last week, how did it go? Encourage them in their discipleship efforts.

❑ Offer a prayer of thanksgiving for God's presence in the week and in the class. Lift up the group's highs and lows and prayer requests. Pray for God's guidance in this time together and along the journey.

❑ Take a few minutes to recall the previous week's word (*glorify*) and lesson. Invite those who were present to contribute to the review. Transition to the lesson (next page) by referring to today's word: *devotion*.

Sending

(5–10 minutes) **Supplies:** *paper or notecards, pens or pencils*

❑ Ask the students to reflect on the lesson. What did they discover about *devotion*? What might devotion to God mean in their lives? What challenges do they face as they seek to follow the path God has prepared? After a minute or so, invite volunteers to tell their thoughts.

❑ As they are ready, have the students write a SMART goal (**S**pecific, **M**easurable, **A**chievable, **R**evealed, and **T**ime limited). Remind them that living SMART is their offering to God for the coming week.

❑ Send the group forth with a blessing of your choosing or say:

> May we stay centered on and devoted to God so that we follow the good path God has prepared for us. In all that we say and do, may our passionate faith show through. Go in peace.

Midweek Checklist

❑ Connect with youth.
❑ Inform parents.
❑ Look over supplies for Option A and supplies and preparation for Option B.

 More About Tending

 *More About Review*

Sample SMART Goal

This week (*time limited*) **I will wear a "devotion bracelet"** (*specific*) **and touch it whenever I need to remind myself of the path God wants me to walk** (*measurable, achievable, and, we trust, revealed to the individual*)**.**

D-E-V-O-T-I-O-N

Busy, Busy, Busy

Put all of the art supplies on a table. Then ask the youth to cut from the magazines and newspapers pictures and large type that represent all of the activities they do or have commitments to do on a regular basis. Then they should glue the cutouts onto their individual posterboard. (Alternative: Instead of creating a montage on posterboard, have the youth turn to page 14 of the bookzine to list their activities and commitments.)

Use the background information on page 20 of this book to introduce the context of today's Scripture lesson. Then announce a "casting call" for a narrator and "a person of great wisdom, strong personality, and dynamic public speaking skills." If you choose to make the "casting call" a real competition, be sensitive to individuals' feelings.

Choose two youth from the casting call. One will read **1 Kings 8:54-55;** the other will read **1 Kings 8:56-61.** Encourage them to read through their parts while you give further instructions to the rest of the youth:

Divide the youth into three teams. Each team will listen with a specific focus in mind:

Team 1: How do you picture Solomon looking as he delivered this speech? Would his body language, gestures, or voice change as he spoke these words?

Team 2: What do these words tell you about the audience's past experience with God?

Team 3: What did Solomon expect from his listeners? Why?

Then give the teams time to discuss their responses, using their Bibles to double-check their findings. Invite the teams to report or, in the case of Team 1, to demonstrate them.

In My Life

(15–20 minutes)

Refer the youth to "What Does Devotion to God Look Like?" (bookzine, page 12). Have the youth work in the small groups or as a class. Have volunteers read aloud the different translations of **1 Kings 8:61a** and then discuss the questions. Then have them write their own version of the verse.

Invite volunteers from the teams to tell about their teams' discussions or to read aloud their version of the verse. Use your own answers to the questions as prompts as needed. Emphasize that devotion to God is an attitude that pervades everything else.

Have the youth work in pairs to look at the posterboard that represents their life (made in the previous activity) and talk with their partner about these questions, which are also printed on page 13 of the bookzine:

• In which activities does your devotion to God show? In what ways?
• Which activities draw your attention away from God?
• How can your devotion to God, your passionate faith, become part of all your activities?

Supplies
• Sheets of posterboard for each participant
• Magazines and newspapers
• Scissors
• Glue
• Markers or crayons
• Pens or pencils
• Bibles
• Bookzines (optional)

Optional Activities

Supplies and Preparation
• Bookzines
• Pens or pencils
• Do this activity in advance yourself so that you can easily add to the discussion.

Music Suggestion

Passciate Faith

Love and Loyalty

(10–20 minutes)

Invite the youth to work on "Passionate Faith" (bookzine, page 14). To whom or what are they devoted? They might include people in their life, causes, commitments, activities—anything that they love and feel loyalty to.

When they've had time to write their list, ask the youth to look at the list and think about where God fits on it. Give them a moment to consider this, then ask:

• You don't have to talk about anything on your list; but as you thought about God, was there anything that surprised you?

Talk about your own list. Explain that devotion to God is part and parcel of our lives. For example, you might say something like, "I am devoted to my family and friends as part of my love for God. My passion for environmental issues comes from my devotion to caring for God's good earth. When I feel devotion for another person, that reflects my devotion to God."

Introduce **1 Kings 8:54-61,** using the background from page 20 of this book. Have a volunteer read the Scripture aloud as everyone else follows along. Point out that Solomon is reminding the people of God's devotion to them: "Not one word has failed of all [God's] good promise" (verse 56).Then reread verse 61 for emphasis.

Let's Get Practical

(15–25 minutes)

Divide the youth into pairs or trios to discuss how devotion to God, a passionate faith in God, might be made known in the situations on page 15 of the bookzine:

• You have to choose how to spend your allowance.
• There's no recycling bin for the soda can you just finished. Do you throw the can in the garbage or take it home with you to recycle there?
• You are considering how to be involved in your faith community—helping with the preschool Sunday school, reading Scripture in worship, folding church newsletters.
• A friend pushes you to do something your parents have forbidden.
• You're out late on Saturday and feel too tired to get up Sunday morning for church.
• You're invited to an afternoon at the arcade or mall (whichever you love more), but you are already signed up for a youth group work day or mission project.
• A friend wants you to give him the answers to a test you took at an earlier period of the same class.

Come together and say something like, "Sometimes it's easy for us to show our devotion to God. At other times, our passionate faith is challenged by peer pressure, the desire not to stand out, conflicting emotions, emotional confusion." Ask:

• What advice would wise Solomon give us? (*Try to stay focused on God, devoted to God, passionate about our faith in God, following the path we've been shown by Jesus.*)

Supplies and Preparation
• Bibles
• Bookzines
• Pens or pencils
• Symbols of your personal passions (For example: Bible, basketball, pot of flowers, photo of your family)
• As preparation for this activity, make your own list of people, things, causes, or activities to which you are devoted; decide how much you would be willing to share with the group.

Supplies
• Bookzines

Movie Suggestion

Beloved

God loves us! We are God's beloved. I am beloved!

1 John 4:7-12 (Beloved, love one another—love is from God.)

Additional Background

Somewhere along this journey we have to recognize and claim the rock-solid truth that God loves us, that we are indeed God's beloved. Otherwise, life is a jumble of activities, a mishmash of ideas, a slippery slope on the way to who-knows-where.

As adults who work with youth, we realize that often many of their struggles go back to the heart questions of Am I loved? and Why would anyone love me? Even young persons who are blessed with loving families and a loving congregation still have at least an ounce of doubt to deal with. And for too many youth, the empty answers are at the bottom of poor behavior and poor choices.

> *Somewhere along this journey, we have to recognize and claim the rock-solid truth that God loves us, that we are indeed God's beloved.*

Transformation and faith maturation come through the answer that, regardless of anything else, we can be sure of God's love for us. That love is not only for us as human beings and as a community of faith but also for each of as individuals. God's love encompasses all of us, but it also reaches down to wrap "loving arms" around each of us. We are beloved!

We are reminded that "neither death, nor life, neither angels, nor rulers, nor things present, nor things to come, nor powers, nor height, nor depth, nor anything else in all creation, will be able to separate us from the love of God in Christ Jesus our Lord" (**Romans 8:38-39**).

Today's Scripture also points to the supreme act of love for us: "God sent his only Son into the world so that we might live through him. In this is love, not that we loved God but that [God] loved us and sent his Son to be the atoning sacrifice for our sins" (**1 John 4:9-10**). God has done the ultimate act to show the depth of love God has for us. We are Christians—not just because we try to live as Jesus taught; but also because, in his willingness to go to the cross for us, we see how deeply God through Christ loves us. God loved us first—just because.

> *Today's Scripture points to the supreme act of love for us.*

God continues to pursue us, showering blessings upon us, forgiving us and giving us second chances, calling us back into relationship, showing us a more excellent way, being with us, helping us always. In so many ways, God shows us love. Love is not just a wonderful feeling. Feelings come and go. Love is a deep-rooted decision as well as the action that backs it up. We experience God's love through other people, through the community of faith, through grace in unexpected ways, through creation, and most especially through Jesus Christ.

Our role is to help the youth recognize and claim the fact that they are God's beloved. Our own relationship with the youth, the love they experience in the Christian community of the class and the congregation, and the experiences of showing love to others are all ways that we help them open their eyes and hearts to God's love for them.

Beloved, love one another. Love is from God; and when we love, God lives in us!

Tending	**A**	**Let Me Count the Ways**	*Sending*
Review Noticing God in Our Week Preview	**B**	— or — **Jesus Loves Me**	Reflection Our Offering to God Blessing

Tending

(10–20 minutes) **Supplies:** *large, white candle; candleholder; matches*

❑ As the youth arrive, welcome them. Light the candle, and invite the youth into this sacred space and time. Begin the "Tending to God and One Another" conversation:
  • Where were they aware of God in their week or in the world?
  • What "highs" (good things) and what "lows" (rough things) did they experience during the week?
  • What prayer requests do they have—either for themselves or on behalf of someone else?

❑ Ask the youth about their SMART goal. If they tried to live out their "offering to God" last week, how did it go? Encourage them in their discipleship efforts.

❑ Offer a prayer of thanksgiving for God's presence in the week and in the class. Lift up the group's highs and lows and prayer requests. Pray for God's guidance in this time together and along the journey.

❑ Take a few minutes to recall the previous week's word (*devotion*) and lesson. Invite those who were present to contribute to the review. Transition to the lesson (next page) by referring to today's word: *beloved*.

Sending

(5–10 minutes) **Supplies:** *paper or notecards, pens or pencils*

❑ Ask the youth to reflect on the lesson. What did they discover? about themselves? about God? about others? After a minute or two invite volunteers to talk about their insights.

❑ As they are ready, have the youth write their SMART goal (**S**pecific, **M**easurable, **A**chievable, **R**evealed, and **T**ime limited). Remind them that living SMART is their offering to God for the coming week.

❑ Send the students forth with a blessing of your choosing. This one is also on page 20 of the bookzine:

> You *are* God's beloved. Claim that as unshakable truth for your life. Live joyfully and share that love with others. Beloved, let us love one another. Go in peace.

Midweek Checklist

❑ Connect with youth.
❑ Inform parents.
❑ Look over supplies and preparation for Option A.

Sample SMART Goal

This week (*time limited*) **every time I doubt that anyone could love me, I will remind myself that I am a beloved child of God; and I will do one action that shows love to someone else** (*specific, measurable, achievable, and, we trust, revealed to the individual*)**.**

Let Me Count the Ways

Supplies and Preparation
- Bookzines
- Pens or pencils
- Markerboard or large sheet of paper
- Markers
- Think of an experience that you want to relate to the class as an example of God's love for you.

Optional Activities

(15–20 minutes)

Direct the youth to "Count the Ways" (bookzine, page 17). Have them work individually and then come together in twos or threes to expand their lists. After a few minutes ask them to report some of the things they identified as ways people show that someone is their beloved.

List these on a markerboard or large sheet of paper. (*They might include such things as being treated with respect, being made to feel special, being included, being complimented and encouraged, seeing that you make the person happy, having the other "be there" when needed, being paid attention to, knowing that the person has made sacrifices to help you, knowing that you are appreciated, knowing that we don't have to keep earning the person's love over and over again.*)

Ask the youth to turn to **1 John 4:7-12** in their Bibles or on page 16 of the bookzine. Have a volunteer read it aloud. Then ask:

- What two ways in this Scripture has God shown that we are God's beloved? (*1. God sent God's Son to be the "atoning sacrifice for our sins"; in other words, at a cost to God, God provided the way for us to be in loving relationship. 2. We didn't love God first and so earn God's love; God loved us first and reached out to us.*)

For this next question, you may need to give a story from your own experience; invite others to tell their stories as well:

- In addition to these two ways, how do you know that God loves us? How have you experienced God's love toward you? (*Other people who love God also show God's love to us; God blesses us in many ways; God's grace gives us second chances even when we don't deserve them; God has created beauty for us to enjoy; God is with us, especially in our hard times.*)

Love Song to God

Supplies
- Bookzines
- Pens or pencils

(15–20 minutes)

Give the youth options for creating a "love song" to God. Have them use page 18 of the bookzine to create lyrics and music, write a poem, make some notes about what they would say or do. The youth may work individually or with a partner. Give them some time for creativity, and reserve some time for "show and tell."

As you summarize, be sure to point out that a key way we show our love in response is to "love one another, because love is from God." We love because God first loved us. Because we are loved, we can love others.

Jesus Loves Me

No Doubt About It!

(15–20 minutes)

Give the youth a few minutes to brainstorm what they know about love. What is love? How would they describe it? What are the qualities of love? Write their responses on a markerboard or large sheet of paper.

Try to engage the youth in singing "Jesus Loves Me." Some of them might not have ever heard it. So if no one knows it well enough to sing it, just refer to the words. Ask them how many of them have heard someone one say, "Jesus loves you." Then ask:

• What do you think it means to say, "Jesus loves me"?

Direct the group to page 16 of the bookzine. Divide the youth into two groups, and have the groups alternate in reading aloud the verses of today's Scripture, **1 John 4:7-12.** Ask:

• What did Jesus do that shows his love? (*Jesus died on the cross to conquer sin so that we can receive God's love.*)
• What did God do? (*God sent God's only Son as a sacrifice to show how great God's love is for us.*)
• What other familiar Scripture do you know that relates to this idea? (***John 3:16***) What do you think that means? (*God loves all of us, including me.*)

So What?

(10–15 minutes)

Direct the youth to "Am I Loved?" (bookzine, page 19). Each youth is to work alone to find a way to illustrate feelings or to create a simile or metaphor for times when he or she feels unloved and for times when he or she knows that he or she is loved. Explain that a *simile* compares two unlike things as if they are similar: "My love *is like* a red, red rose" (Robert Burns) or "I am sending you out *like* lambs into the midst of wolves" (Luke 10:3b). A *metaphor* uses a word or phrase that usually stands for one thing to stand for another: "My love *is* a rose" or "The Lord *is* my shepherd" (Psalm 23:1a).

After a few minutes, invite the youth to tell about their creations. Invite volunteers to demonstrate with their whole body what those experiences feel like. For example, feeling unloved might be shown by curling up tightly; or looking down; or putting hands in front of one's face, palms out, as if to hide. Feeling beloved might be arms open, or looking up smiling, or even turning cart wheels. Ask:

• Why is being loved so important? What would the world be like without love?
• What difference does it make in our lives to know that we are God's beloved sons and daughters?
• How can knowing that we are loved help us as we relate to other people? (*Since we are loved, we also ought to love one another, especially as a witness to the world.*)

Remind the youth that even though God is the great Creator of all, even though God knows and sees everything, God loves us as human beings *and* as individuals. We can claim the truth of God's love for us and live joyfully.

Supplies
• Bookzines
• Pens or pencils
• Markerboard or large sheet of paper
• Markers

Music Suggestions

Supplies
• Bookzines
• Pens or pencils

Decision

We choose to follow Jesus through the large and small decisions we make each day.

Luke 5:1-11 (The fishermen decide to follow Jesus.)

Additional Background

The Sea of Galilee is, in reality, little more than a very large lake—only eight miles wide and thirteen miles long. With numerous species of fish found in its waters, the area was and is still known for its fishing industry. Jesus made his home along the north shore of the sea during the time of his ministry and spent quite a bit of time there.

Luke 5:1-11 takes place there. The scene was routine, the fishermen cleaning their nets, except that Jesus was there too. A crowd had gathered and wanted the rabbi to teach them; so he asked permission from Simon, one of the fishermen, to take a boat a little way from shore where he could speak without being surrounded by the crowd.

When Jesus finished teaching, he instructed Simon (who later became Peter) to put the boat out in the water and go back to fishing. Simon complained that they had been fishing all night long. More than likely they were tired and wanted nothing more than to go to bed. Certainly their nets were cleaned and were drying in the sun. If they went back to fishing, they would have to clean the nets all over again.

Christ calls people to be followers no matter how they see themselves.

For some reason, Simon rose above his complaints, went back into deep water, and put his nets down again. Did he know Jesus before this? Had he listened to the teacher at other times? Certainly the others clustered around knew about Jesus. At any rate, Simon went fishing and, as the Scripture says, they caught so many fish that the nets were beginning to break. Simon called for help; his partners in another boat came to the rescue. They filled both boats so full that the boats were in danger of sinking.

Simon fell before Jesus and begged him to leave; for, as he said, "I am a sinful man!" In the presence of this unique man, Simon recognized his own unworthiness. Yet Jesus saw something special in Simon and invited him to be a follower. Then something unusual happened. When they returned to shore, Simon, James, and John left their careers and their boats behind. They walked away from all they knew to follow Jesus.

During their early teen years, youth are developing a new self-image. Trying to figure out how they measure up in their world can be hard on them. Very often, they wrestle with feelings of not being good enough. One message from this Scripture is that Christ calls people to be followers no matter how they see themselves. Christ sees the good and the potential in all of us, and invites us to a life of service.

Youth make a whole series of less heart-stopping decisions every week, which add up over time; each decision can be an indicator of whether they are choosing to follow Jesus.

Simon's decision to leave nets and boats and career behind was huge. Most youth don't often make this kind of momentous choice. They do, however, make a whole series of less heart-stopping decisions every week, which add up over time; each one can be an indicator of whether they are choosing to follow Jesus or go another way.

Youth need opportunities from time to time to encounter the decision whether to follow Jesus. Such an occasion is offered during the Sending this week. It is important to offer the invitation with the passion you feel but also without making the youth feel pressured to do something they find uncomfortable.

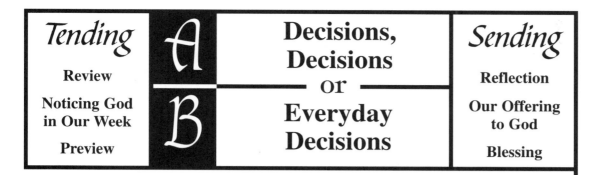

Tending	A⁄B	Decisions, Decisions — or — Everyday Decisions	Sending
Review Noticing God in Our Week Preview			Reflection Our Offering to God Blessing

Tending

(10–20 minutes) **Supplies:** *large, white candle; candleholder; matches*

❑ As the youth arrive, welcome them. Light the candle, and invite the youth into this sacred space and time. Begin the "Tending to God and One Another" conversation:
   - Where were they aware of God in their week or in the world?
   - What "highs" (good things) and what "lows" (rough things) did they experience during the week?
   - What prayer requests do they have—either for themselves or on behalf of someone else?

❑ Ask the youth about their SMART goal. If they tried to live out their "offering to God" last week, how did it go? Encourage them in their discipleship efforts.

❑ Offer a prayer of thanksgiving for God's presence in the week and in the class. Lift up the group's highs and lows and prayer requests. Pray for God's guidance in this time together and along the journey.

❑ Take a few minutes to recall the previous week's word (*beloved*) and lesson. Invite those who were present to contribute to the review. Transition to the lesson (next page) by referring to today's word: *decision*.

Sending

(5–10 minutes) **Supplies:** *paper or notecards, pens or pencils. (Optional: Put a cross or a fishing net in the worship center.)*

❑ (*Options*) Follow the usual pattern for this time or use this idea: Ask the youth to remember the fishermen's decision to follow Jesus. Invite the youth to spend a moment in silent prayer. Then if they are willing to follow Jesus, have them write, "I choose Jesus," on their card and fold the card in half. If they are not willing to take this step, let them write any thought they wish (or leave the cards blank) and fold them in half. When they are ready, invite them to tape their decisions to the cross (or attach them to the fish net).

❑ As they are ready, have the students write a SMART goal (**S**pecific, **M**easurable, **A**chievable, **R**evealed, and **T**ime limited). Remind them that living SMART is their offering to God for the coming week.

❑ Send the group forth with this blessing:

   Jesus invites us, "Come, follow me." May your decision bless you for the rest of your life and beyond. Go in peace.

Midweek Checklist

❑ Connect with youth.
❑ Inform parents.
❑ Look over supplies and preparation for Option A.

Sample SMART Goal

By tomorrow (*time limited*) **I will decide** (*measurable*) **whether to participate in the CROP Walk scheduled for next weekend** (*specific, achievable and, we trust, revealed to the individual*)**.**

Decisions, Decisions

Fruit Cones

Supplies and Preparation
- Various fruits
- Ice cream cones
- Yogurt
- Chocolate syrup
- Honey
- Spoons
- Small bowls
- Scrap paper
- Pens or pencils
- Ahead of time, gather and prepare the fruit, ice cream cones, and other supplies. Cut the fruit up into small pieces. Put each type of fruit in a separate bowl. Arrange all of the food and supplies on a table.

(15–25 minutes)

Let the youth make fruit cones. They will select the fruit to place in their cones. They can layer the fruit with yogurt, chocolate syrup, or honey. If they do not wish to use ice cream cones, they may use a small bowl.

Ground rule: The youth must count the number of decisions they make in creating their fruit cones; have them each keep a tally on a piece of scrap paper.

Talk about what happened as the youth eat their fruit cones. Ask:

- How many decisions did you make?
- Were these easy choices?
- How many decisions do you think you make during a normal day?
- How many big decisions do you think you make during a normal week?

The Choice

(10–25 minutes)

Divide the youth into three groups, then read aloud **Luke 5:1-11.** Ask the youth to imagine that they are Peter. As you read the Scripture again, Group 1 will imagine what Peter *sees* at each stage of the story; Group 2 will focus on what Peter *hears*; and a third group will concentrate on what emotions Peter *feels*.

Have the youth close their eyes as you read the Scripture slowly. Then let the groups talk among themselves about their assignment for about three minutes before reporting their findings to the rest of the class. Then ask:

- What did you discover by listening to Scripture this way?
- Do you think that Peter knew Jesus before this day?
- What, do you think, was so compelling about Jesus that these men left everything to follow him?
- What is there about Jesus that would make people want to follow him nowadays?
- Peter felt totally unworthy of even being in Jesus' presence. Yet Jesus asked Peter to follow him. Do you think that people still feel that way? What does it mean to follow Jesus, even when you don't feel worthy enough?

Turn the conversation to the decisions of the youth. Ask:

- Have you been confirmed, or have you made a decision to be a Christian?
- If so, how hard was it to make that choice? What made it easy or hard?

Refer them to your church's confirmation or baptism ritual. (A sample is on the website.) Read the questions aloud, and talk about what they mean. Point out that the decision Peter and the others made that day sent them in a particular direction. But every day afterward was filled with decisions to continue to follow, to continue to be faithful.

Optional Activities

Supplies
- Bibles
- Copies of your church's baptism or confirmation ritual, or printouts from *www.claimthelife.com*

Everyday Decisions

That Many?!

(10–15 minutes)

Supplies
• Markerboard or large sheet of paper
• Markers

Ask the youth to think of everything they did since getting up in the morning and to estimate how many decisions they made during that time. Encourage them to think of both major and minor decisions. Record their numbers; average the results. Then estimate what percentage of their waking hours has taken place; use that number to estimate how many decisions they will make today. For example, if the average number of decisions is 50, and one-fourth (0.25) of the day is over, they might make an average of 200 decisions today (50 decisions multiplied by 4 = 200). Ask:

• Does this number surprise you? Why, or why not?
• How many of your decisions a day do you think reflect your values or faith? Give some examples from a typical or recent day.

Guidelines for Decisions

(20–25 minutes)

Supplies
• Bibles
• Bookzines
• Pens or pencils
• Paper

Divide the youth into three groups. Assign each group one of the situations on page 22 of the bookzine. Have someone from each group read aloud **Luke 5:1-11** while the others follow along in their Bibles. Give the groups several minutes to discuss how the people in their scenario would react to the situations. Ask them to improvise a skit about what they think would be said and done by their characters and then present the skit to the rest of the group. After the groups have presented their skits, ask:

• What did you discover about this Scripture as you prepared for your skit?
• How risky was the decision that Peter, James, and John made?
• How did the reactions of the people in these skits compare with reactions people often make in the face of big decisions?

Explain that many of our decisions large and small set the direction of our lives. But sometimes we struggle to know which decisions are in line with being followers of Jesus. Here is one helpful set of guidelines to use in big and small, everyday decisions we face: Invite the group to read **Philippians 4:8** (bookzine, page 23) in unison.

Hymn Suggestions

Have the youth work together or in smaller groups. Ask them to read the dilemma on page 24 of the bookzine or use a real-life situation that one of the youth is facing or that is suggested. They are to list a series of choices the person could make. Then they will select one choice and evaluate it against the guidelines given in Philippians.

As the groups report, encourage them to show how they used the passage as criteria for making a decision.

Disciple

Being a disciple means putting God first in every way, above what we have and what we want, and even above our family and friends.

Luke 14:25-33 (Discipleship has a cost.)

> "Whoever comes to me and does not hate father and mother, wife and children, brothers and sisters, yes, and even life itself, cannot be my disciple. Whoever does not carry the cross and follow me cannot be my disciple."—**Luke 14:26-27**

 *Additional Background*

This passage is shocking at first read. How could Jesus say that anyone wanting to be his disciple must hate every family member and even life itself? In this passage the word *hate* is not literal but a metaphor for prioritizing family within the greater priority of following Christ. Throughout the Bible, Jesus teaches the primacy of love, even loving enemies; so the use of this word emphasizes that our discipleship comes first. Our relationship with Christ should be put above all other relationships and loyalties.

In **Matthew 10:37-38,** Jesus speaks on the same subject, clarifying the hate passage:

We can't make bargains with God or put conditions on our loyalty.

> "Whoever loves father or mother more than me is not worthy of me;
> and whoever loves son or daughter more than me is not worthy of me."

Jesus doesn't mean that we shouldn't love our families. He does mean that we should never love anyone or anything more than we love God. This instruction seems so simple, yet it can be so very hard to carry out. Perhaps, if we could comprehend the enormity of how much God loves us, we might find it easier for our love of God to take priority in our lives.

How do we help teens understand what this priority can mean for their lives? We can guide them toward making the decision to live for Christ above all else, especially since teens often find themselves in a world that points to self-gratification and satisfying their own wants and desires first.

We are asked to give up the things that separate us from God.

As followers of Jesus, we may give up much. Jesus is clear about that. We can't make bargains with God or put conditions on our loyalties. Jesus gave us the conditions of discipleship. Living as disciples involves some level of sacrifice in order to turn our hearts wholly toward God. We are asked to give up the things that separate us from God, things such as relationships, material possessions, habits, attitudes, pride, choices, or more.

During the conversations about discipleship, encourage the youth to explore ways they can make choices in their lives that put God first, choices that reflect life in Christ. Help the youth consider what the cost of discipleship is for them personally—and remind them of the rewards too. When we are in right relationship with God (loving God above all else), then all else is right too.

Tending	A/B	Can You Carry It? or First Things First	Sending
Review Noticing God in Our Week Preview			Reflection Our Offering to God Blessing

Tending

(10–20 minutes) **Supplies:** *large, white candle; candleholder; matches*

❏ As the youth arrive, welcome them. Light the candle, and invite the youth into this sacred space and time. Begin the "Tending to God and One Another" conversation:
  - Where were they aware of God in their week or in the world?
  - What "highs" (good things) and what "lows" (rough things) did they experience during the week?
  - What prayer requests do they have—either for themselves or on behalf of someone else?

❏ Ask the youth about their SMART goal. If they tried to live out their "offering to God" last week, how did it go? Encourage them in their discipleship efforts.

❏ Offer a prayer of thanksgiving for God's presence in the week and in the class. Lift up the group's highs and lows and prayer requests. Pray for God's guidance in this time together and along the journey.

❏ Take a few minutes to recall the previous week's word (*decision*) and lesson. Invite those who were present to contribute to the review. Transition to the lesson (next page) by referring to today's word: *disciple*.

Sending

(5–10 minutes) **Supplies:** *paper or notecards, pens or pencils*

❏ Allow time for the youth to reflect silently on the lesson. What did they discover about being a disciple? What has become clear to them? What important things were they reminded of? What new things did they realize? Invite volunteers to share their thoughts.

❏ As they are ready, have the youth write a SMART goal (**S**pecific, **M**easurable, **A**chievable, **R**evealed, and **T**ime limited). Remind them that living SMART is their offering to God for the coming week.

❏ Send the group forth with a blessing of your choosing or use this simple reminder:

> May you discover that life in Christ is worth the cost of discipleship. Go in peace.

Midweek Checklist

❏ Connect with youth.
❏ Inform parents.
❏ Look over supplies and preparation for Option A and supplies for Option B.

Sample SMART Goal

This week (*time limited*) **I will give up at least one thing** (*measurable*) **in order to focus more fully on God in my life** (*specific, achievable, and, we trust, revealed to the individual*)**.**

Can You Carry It?

The Cross

(20–25 minutes)

Supplies

- 2 standard length 2-by-4 boards of lumber or thin logs
- Pencils
- Measuring tapes
- 8 or more 3-inch nails
- 2 hammers
- Wood saws

Optional Supplies

- Rope
- Christmas tree stand
- Roll or large sheets of paper
- Markers

Supplies

- Bibles
- Bookzines
- Pens or pencils
- 3 Small pieces of paper for each person

Optional Activities

If possible, have the group work together to build a cross. Encourage them to use their imaginations as they feel the wood and as they hear the sound of the nails being driven into the wood.

The cross should be at least 5 feet tall, made from 2-by-4 lumber or thin logs. Measure the wood, and cut off one third to use as the horizontal piece. The remaining two thirds will be the vertical piece. Nail them together, or lash criss-cross with rope to create a cross. Cut another 2-by-4 into 4 equal pieces to make a stand for the cross, or use a Christmas tree stand. (Easy Alternative: Draw and color in a large cross on butcher paper or some other large paper, or line up several sheets of paper to make the shape of a cross. Attach the cross drawing to the wall.)

Follow Me

(10–15 minutes)

Point out to the group that dying on the cross was the price Jesus paid for following God's will. In today's Scripture, Jesus says that there are costs to those of us, too, who would follow him as disciples.

Direct the youth to find **Luke 14:25-33** in their Bibles. Invite a volunteer to read the passage aloud as the others follow along. Tell the group that the word *hate* does not have the same meaning as we usually give it. Rather, here it is used to set up a contrast with what or whom we should love more.

- Whom are we to love more than we love our family? (*Jesus, God*)
- We're also supposed to give up our possessions in order to be Jesus' disciples. Why, do you think, would Jesus make such a demand? (*Because it's easy for us to start loving our things more than we love Christ.*)
- We have to "carry our cross" in order to be Jesus' disciple. What does a cross symbolize? (*Suffering and death, which may be what a disciple has to face.*)

Have the youth work together in pairs or trios. Distribute 3 small slips of paper and a pen or pencil to each person. Instruct the group to write at the top of one slip the word *stuff*; at the top of the second, *me*; and at the top of the third, *others*. These are also noted at the bottom of page 28 in the bookzine.

Direct the pairs or trios to "Hearts Wholly Toward God" (bookzine, page 28) for their reflection. Tell them to discuss the questions if they are comfortable doing so, then each person is to write something that he or she feels the need to give up or balance in order to put God first in relation to "stuff," "self," and "others." When they finish writing their responses, ask them to fold the slips and put them on the cross. Refer them to page 29 for personal prayer.

- What, do you think, will God do with the needs we have taken to the cross?

First Things First

B

So Much Stuff!

(15–25 minutes)

Ask for two volunteers to read to the group. Load one of them up with all kinds of things—a variety of items that represents today's busy life. Then hand them both their bookzine, and have them read aloud the dialogue on page 26. The one without the armload reads first, as "A." The one with the armload, "B," has to keep holding all of the stuff while reading. If anything drops, put it back on top of the stack. Then ask:

- What do you think would have happened if (*insert A's name*) had invited (*insert B's name*) to travel around with (*insert* him *or* her)?
- If (*insert B's name*) were to agree, how long do you think that arrangement would last? Why?
- When have you agreed to do something and then found that you just had too much going on to take on one more thing? What was that experience like?
- Did you know in advance what might be required of you? If you had known more, how would that have affected your decision?

Point out to the youth that often when a person wants someone else to do something, that person is tempted to do a sales job, selling only the good aspects of the task, leaving out the cost. Not so with Jesus. This passage is often called "The Cost of Discipleship." Direct the youth to find **Luke 14:25-33** in their Bible. Invite a volunteer to read it aloud as the group follows along. Then ask:

- What does Jesus indicate might stand in the way of being fully devoted disciples? (*love of family and life, not "carrying the cross," having possessions*)
- Why, do you think, would Jesus talk about "hating" your family? Wasn't he the one who told us to love others, even our enemies? (*Jesus is indicating priorities: Loving God and following Jesus are more important than even our families. We have to be wholly committed to do what Jesus calls us to if we are to be disciples and not just admirers in the crowd.*)
- What, do you think, did Jesus mean by his reference to "carrying the cross"? (*Christians throughout the ages have suffered in many ways because they have chosen to follow Jesus. Being a Christian does not always mean an easy life.*)
- What connections do you see between this Scripture and the opening skit?

Putting God First

(5–10 minutes)

Say: Living as disciples involves some level of sacrifice in order to turn our hearts wholly toward God. We are asked to give up anything that separates us from God. Those things might be relationships, material possessions, habits, attitudes, pride, choices, and so on. What will it cost *you* to be a disciple?

Refer the youth to "More on the Word" (bookzine, page 27) for personal reflection. Give the group time to write their responses. Then invite the youth to silently pray the prayer on page 29.

Supplies
- Bibles
- Bookzines
- Pens or pencils
- A variety of items that represent today's busy life, such as a phone, school books or a large dictionary, clothing, sports equipment, purse, backpack, drinking cup

Supplies
- Bookzines
- Pens or pencils

Abstain

 *Additional Background*

Abstinence is a word that has gained a great deal of significance in recent years as we have debated what type of sex education is best for children and youth in our country. Because of this debate, the word is primarily associated with sex. While God's gift of sexuality is an area of significance, it is not the only issue where today's teens should consider being abstinent.

The Scripture for this session provides a significant list of activities, behaviors, and attitudes where wise and prudent decision-making would suggest that abstinence is the best choice. While the list is amazingly complete, in numerous other situations the choice of abstaining could enhance life rather than limit it, especially when we consider our identity as part of God's good creation and as followers of Jesus. "Other wild and evil things" probably cover most of those, and in this session the youth will have opportunities to identify more that are specific to them.

Abstinence is not about what we can't do but about who we are called to be as followers of Jesus.

The term *abstain* has also been cast in a negative light by those to whom it applies in a given situation. They view the prohibition as "stopping me from doing what I really want to do." The directive to abstain also provokes some people to legalism. They focus their energy on what they can get by with without actually crossing a particular line. For example, some teens interpret sexual abstinence to mean that they can participate in any physical activity with a partner that doesn't include intercourse.

The Scripture passage gives us the basis we need to provide our students with a more positive way of looking at abstinence. It is not about what we can't do but about who we are called to be as followers of Jesus. It is about living in the Spirit. It is about exhibiting the presence of God in all of our actions and interactions.

Abstinence gives us room in our lives to explore Spirit-filled living, without the baggage of hurt from involvement in negative activities.

Abstaining from activities that rob us of some measure of our selfhood provides us with the opportunity to live our lives in other, more meaningful ways—ways that give life rather than taking it. We are able to see the world, others, even ourselves in a way that affirms who we are and Whose we are. We have room in our lives to explore Spirit-filled living without the baggage of hurt from involvement in negative activities. Abstinence is not primarily about the activity but about how the activity affects relationships—with ourselves, with others, with God, and with our world.

Please recognize that in any gathering of youth, the potential is high for you to have teenagers who have experienced or are experiencing situations that Scripture and Christian practice would say are inappropriate. Your group may include youth who are using alcohol or drugs, gossiping, engaging in sexual activity, smoking. You can talk about the topic of abstinence in relation to any of these. You also need to talk about God's grace and forgiveness—the opportunity to start over. This focus is built into the session plan; your sensitivity to those in your group can help you know how to include those aspects in a meaningful way.

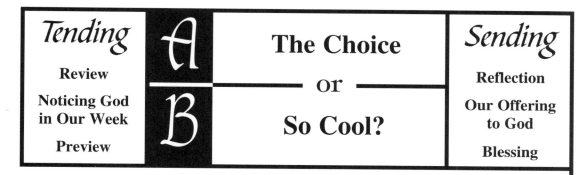

Tending

(10–20 minutes) **Supplies:** *large, white candle; candleholder; matches*

❑ As the youth arrive, welcome them. Light the candle, and invite the youth into this sacred space and time. Begin the "Tending to God and One Another" conversation:
  • Where were they aware of God in their week or in the world?
  • What "highs" (good things) and what "lows" (rough things) did they experience during the week?
  • What prayer requests do they have—either for themselves or on behalf of someone else?

❑ Ask the youth about their SMART goal. If they tried to live out their "offering to God" last week, how did it go? Encourage them in their discipleship efforts.

❑ Offer a prayer of thanksgiving for God's presence in the week and in the class. Lift up the group's highs and lows and prayer requests. Pray for God's guidance in this time together and along the journey.

❑ Take a few minutes to recall the previous week's word (*disciple*) and lesson. Invite those who were present to contribute to the review. Transition to the lesson (next page) by referring to today's word: *abstain*.

Sending

(5–10 minutes) **Supplies:** *paper or notecards, pens or pencils*

❑ Ask the youth to reflect on the lesson. What surprised them? What was new to them? Invite them to consider areas in their lives where abstaining would make more room for God's Spirit.

❑ As they are ready, have the youth write a SMART goal (**S**pecific, **M**easurable, **A**chievable, **R**evealed, and **T**ime limited). Remind them that living SMART is their offering to God for the coming week.

❑ Send the group forth with the following blessing or another one of your choosing:

> Go from here with God's grace to choose to live in ways that make more room for God's Spirit. Abstain from those things that fill your God-space with the negative. Go in peace.

Midweek Checklist

❑ Connect with youth.
❑ Inform parents.
❑ Look over supplies and preparation for Option A; or have on hand *Veracity Video Vignettes, Volume 3,* for Option B.

Sample SMART Goal

Each night this week (*time limited*) **I will reflect on my day and try to identify when my desires have overshadowed my relationship with God** (*specific*)**. I will identify at least one area where I need to practice abstinence** (*measurable, achievable, and, we trust, revealed to the individual*)**.**

The Choice

Follow That Desire!

Supplies and Preparation
- Markerboards or large sheets of paper
- Markers
- Masking tape
- Write "desires" on one large sheet of paper and "outcomes" on the second. Hang them on the wall.

(10 minutes)

Ask for two volunteers to be scribes and to record the work of the group. Direct everyone to **Galatians 5:16-21,** printed on page 30 of the bookzine. Invite one or two volunteers to read the Scripture aloud.

Then have the group create a list of all of the behaviors that people's selfish desires lead them to (identified in the passage). Both scribes can take turns writing to shorten the time for this task. Be sure to help the group with definitions if they are not sure what a term means.

Ask the youth to look at the lists and consider whether other activities should be included. Then have the group choose one of the activities. Then ask:

• What are the possible outcomes of giving in to this behavior or activity?

Have the scribes list the outcomes. Then ask:

• If a person chooses to abstain from this selfish desire, rather than giving in to it, what are the likely benefits?

Have the scribes make another list.

Point/Counterpoint

Optional Supplies
- Videocamera and videotape or DVD
- VCR or DVD player
- TV

(30 minutes)

Divide the group into two teams. Have each team develop a story line and "movie" for a character. One team's main character will choose to give in to desire and negative behavior; the other team's main character will choose to abstain from the activity.

Give the groups about 20 minutes to develop their "movies." Explain that all of the members of the group must be a part of the movie production. Then come back together and have each team perform its movie. (Optional: Record the movies with a videocamera, then show the movies to the group.)

Optional Activity

Say: "We've had the opportunity to act out two scenarios as they relate to our human desires and how we respond to them—one about giving in; one about abstaining from the negative activity. Choices about how we will live—by our own desires or by the Spirit's leading—confront us on an ongoing basis. I have two points that I want you to have in your head as we wrap up our time together:

✔ First, choosing to abstain from a negative or inappropriate activity is not so much about giving up something; rather it is a decision to live more fully in God's Spirit.

✔ Second, we all choose not to abstain and give in to some human desire at some point in our lives. The good news is that God's grace allows us to recognize those negative choices, ask for forgiveness, and start over again.

So Cool?

You're Not the Only One

(20–25 minutes)

Ask the youth what immediately comes to mind when they hear the words *abstain* or *abstinence*. Have them "popcorn" their responses, saying them quickly.

Show the video "So Cool?" Then direct the youth to "So Cool?" (bookzine, page 31). If your group is large, divide the youth into smaller ones for discussion. Have volunteers use the questions in the bookzine to facilitate the discussion within their group. (Taking on this assignment can help them develop leadership skills.)

Bring the groups together again. Invite each group to report on the question that generated the liveliest discussion. Ask follow-up questions to stimulate more discussion.

Supplies
- Bibles
- *Veracity Video Vignettes, Volume 3,* ("So Cool?")
- DVD player and TV
- Bookzines
- Pens or pencils

Does It Matter?

(10–15 minutes)

Direct the youth to **Galatians 5:16-21,** printed on page 30 of the bookzine. Invite a volunteer to read the Scripture aloud while the others follow along.

Instruct the youth to respond to the checklist on pages 32–33 of the bookzine. Then ask:

- What did you observe in doing this checklist? (*Most actions by an individual create suffering beyond just that person, often beyond even the person's family.*)

Encourage the youth to give examples of ways people might suffer as a result of the behaviors listed on page 32. Remind the youth that God cares about all of us, individually and as a community. Abstaining from some things is a way of our loving our neighbors, as we are called to do. Our focus is not on giving up something but rather on choosing the positive.

Supplies
- Bookzines
- Pens or pencils
- Small pieces of paper or index cards

Give each youth a small piece of paper. Ask the youth to write one area of desire where they have chosen to practice abstinence. Then ask them to write another area where they need to make a decision about abstinence (a place where they are not currently abstaining from an activity, such as smoking, or an area where they really hadn't thought about abstinence before, such as making hurtful comments to or about others). Invite volunteers to talk about either answer. To encourage openness, keep your tone invitational, for example: Can you tell us more about why that choice is important to you? What would cause you to make a different choice? Do not ask specific youth to respond; respect their choice to skip the sharing. Encourage the youth to put the scraps of paper away and to think more in the week to come about their choices related to abstinence.

Say: "I want you to have in your head two things as we wrap up our time together. One is that, in abstaining from a negative or inappropriate activity, we make room for God's Spirit to work in our lives. The second is that we will, all at some time, give in to human desire. The good news is that God's grace helps us recognize those negative choices, ask for forgiveness, and start over again."

Love

In Christ we are free—not to do whatever pleases us—but to love our neighbors as ourselves.

Galatians 5:13-14 (The whole law summed up: "Love your neighbor.")

Additional Background

Have you ever played "Who's Your Neighbor?" In this fun, youth group game, everyone sits in a circle, with one person sitting in the middle. The middle person points at someone and asks, "Who are your neighbors?" After the chosen person gives the names of the persons to his or her left and right, the middle person asks, "Who would you like to be your neighbors?" The two persons named first must jump up and switch places with the "like-to-be-neighbors." Temporary chaos reigns as five people (the middle person also tries to gain a spot) scramble to find a place to sit. The person without a seat in the circle becomes the next middle person.

This game helps everyone learn one another's names but also raises a crucial question that we must answer in order to understand this week's Scripture passage: Who is my neighbor?

One answer would be that our neighbors are those who live next to us or, at least, in our neighborhood. This narrow geographical answer doesn't fit with Jesus' response to the lawyer who asked what he needed to do to inherit eternal life (**Luke 10:25-37**). Jesus told the story of the good Samaritan to illustrate how an unexpected person (the Samaritan, a traditional enemy of the Jews) was the real neighbor because he "showed mercy" to the man who had fallen into the hands of robbers.

> *So, our neighbors can be next door or across the world. We may know our neighbors personally or never meet them, or we may even be considered enemies.*

So, our neighbors can be next door or across the world. We may know our neighbors personally or never meet them, or we may even consider them our enemies. When Paul reminds the Galatians, "The whole law is summed up in a single commandment, 'You shall love your neighbor as yourself' " (5:14), he is quoting the response Jesus gave when asked what the most important commandment was (**Mark 12:28-34**).

Observant Jews were well aware of the commandments. They knew that Moses had given what is called "The Great Commandment" (**Deuteronomy 6:1-9**). Verses 4-5, known as the *Shema* (or "Hear!"), are still an intrinsic part of the everyday Jewish prayer life:

> "Hear, O Israel: The LORD is our God, the LORD alone. You shall love the LORD your God with all your heart, and with all your soul, and with all your might."

> *Freedom as the freedom to love and serve others may be a new concept for teens.*

However, Jesus adds on to the Great Commandment: "The second is this: 'You shall love your neighbor as yourself' " (**Mark 12:31**). Paul emphasizes this key concept again in **Ephesians 5:13-14,** urging the followers of Jesus to "use your freedom to serve one another in love: that's how freedom grows" (*The Message*). Using the word *freedom* to mean "the freedom to love and serve others" may be a new concept for teens. After we explore these ideas, the youth will better understand the connections among love, freedom, and serving.

Tending

(10–20 minutes) **Supplies:** *large, white candle; candleholder; matches*

❏ As the youth arrive, welcome them. Light the candle, and invite the youth into this sacred space and time. Begin the "Tending to God and One Another" conversation:
  - Where were they aware of God in their week or in the world?
  - What "highs" (good things) and what "lows" (rough things) did they experience during the week?
  - What prayer requests do they have—either for themselves or on behalf of someone else?

❏ Ask the youth about their SMART goal. If they tried to live out their "offering to God" last week, how did it go? Encourage them in their discipleship efforts.

❏ Offer a prayer of thanksgiving for God's presence in the week and in the class. Lift up the group's highs and lows and prayer requests. Pray for God's guidance in this time together and along the journey.

❏ Take a few minutes to recall the previous week's word (*abstain*) and lesson. Invite those who were present to contribute to the review. Transition to the lesson (next page) by referring to today's word: *love*.

Sending

(5–10 minutes) **Supplies:** *paper or notecards, pens or pencils; fabric or ribbons (optional)*

❏ Invite the group to reflect silently on what loving service might look like in their life. Has anything become clear to them? Is there anything they might do differently if service to others were a priority? Does "freedom" have a new meaning for them?

❏ As they are ready, have the students write a SMART goal (**S**pecific, **M**easurable, **A**chievable, **R**evealed, and **T**ime limited). Remind them that living SMART is their offering to God for the coming week.

❏ You could buy fabric to cut into strips, or use ribbon or cord that is long enough to drape around each person's neck as a symbol of the "servant's stole." Hand out these stoles for them to display someplace in their room as a reminder of their call to and freedom in loving service.

❏ Send the group out with this blessing or another one of your choice:

> In Christ we are free—not to do whatever pleases us but to love our neighbors as ourselves. That is true freedom. Go in peace.

Midweek Checklist

❏ Connect with youth.
❏ Inform parents.

Sample SMART Goal

This week (*time limited*) **I will find or create ways to show love to at least three** (*measurable*) **of these:**
1) God,
2) neighbor,
3) self,
4) others, and
5) enemies. I will also write down how I feel after doing so (*specific, attainable, and, we trust, revealed to the individual*)**.**

Real Love

What Do You Know by Heart?

Supplies
• Bookzines
• Pens and pencils

(15–20 minutes)

Challenge the group to recall all Ten Commandments. They may help one another. Chances are, though, you won't have many teens who can do all ten by themselves. (Can you?) Point out that, although the Ten Commandments are special in the Jewish faith and important to the Christian faith, not everyone has them memorized. That may have also been true in Jesus' time, but every observant Jew would have known the Great Commandment. Ask the youth whether they know it.

Ask a volunteer to read aloud **Deuteronomy 6:4-9,** the Great Commandment. Then read verses 4-5 aloud, with the youth repeating these phrases after you:

> Hear, O Israel:
> The LORD is our God, the LORD alone.
> You shall love the LORD your God
> With all your heart,
> And with all your soul,
> And with all your might.

Optional Activities

Repeat this process three or four times, then see whether the whole group you can say these verses together by memory. Say something like, "These are important verses for us to know by heart."

Invite the youth to write their responses to "Heart, Soul, Mind" (bookzine, page 36). Ask them to call out some of their definitions.

Have a volunteer read aloud **Mark 12:28-34.** Then ask:

• What does this passage have in common with the Deuteronomy verses?
• Why might Jesus have added the second Great Commandment?
• How does the second commandment relate to the first? to the Ten Commandments?
• Who is one's neighbor? (*Encourage the youth to recall the story of the good Samaritan.*)

Say, "You shall love your neighbor as yourself." Then ask the youth to repeat it with you.

Paul Adds His Take

Supplies
• Bookzines
• Pens or pencils

(15–20 minutes)

Explain that Paul, the writer of this letter to the churches in Galatia, was an observant Jew. Ask what commandment Paul would have known by heart (*the Great Commandment*). And once Paul began to follow Jesus, what else would he have known by heart? (*Answers should include "Love your neighbor."*)

Read **Galatians 5:13-14** in unison from *The Message* translation, printed on page 34 of the bookzine. Invite the youth to work alone or in pairs or trios to fill in "More Than Virtual Love" (bookzine, page 37). Then have the youth report their ideas to the class.

Who's My Neighbor?

Free to Be

(15–20 minutes)

Supplies
• Bookzines
• Pens or pencils

Ask the youth to choose which statements under "Free to Be" (bookzine, page 38) they believe define the word *freedom*. Then read each statement aloud and have participants raise their hands if they had checked that statement.

Invite a volunteer to read **Galatians 5:13-14** in unison from *The Message* translation, printed on page 34 of the bookzine. Then ask:

• How might Paul define *freedom*?
• Does his definition connect to any of the statements under "Free to Be"?
• What does Paul mean when he says, "Don't use this freedom as an excuse to do whatever you want to do and destroy your freedom"?
• How does loving others increase freedom?
• How do you feel about being given freedom by God? Do the words of George Bernard Shaw, "Liberty means responsibility," make sense?

Get Specific

(15–20 minutes)

Supplies
• Bookzines
• Pens or pencils

Paul says, "An act of true freedom" is "to love others as you love yourself." Ask the youth to call out some definitions of *love*.

Ask for volunteers to read the quotations on page 35 of the bookzine.

Invite participants to hold up one hand as you explain that love is so big there's not any one definition or way of showing love. Start with the thumb, then fold each finger down as you call off five important types of love: 1) love for God; 2) love for neighbor; 3) love for self; 4) love for others; 5) love for enemies. Repeat these five and ask youth to name them off with you as you wiggle or touch each finger in turn.

There are many ways to live out these five kinds of love. Ask the youth to turn to "Get Specific" (bookzine, page 39). Then encourage them to call out ways to show love.

For instance, you could write *show respect* as one way of showing love. In which categories might *show respect* work? (*All five, although that respect might look different, depending on whether you were respecting yourself, God, or other people.*) Then the youth may write *show respect*. (*Some other possibilities: Listen to another's problems; try to see things from another's perspective.*)

Give the group time to fill in their specifics. Remind the youth that any of these could be used in their SMART goal for the week. Invite conversations about their ideas.

Action

Followers of Christ are called to faithful, loving action—not just words.

1 John 3:16-18 (Let us love in truth and action.)

 *Additional Background*

God not only says that God loves humanity; God shows it.

Our talk of love for God should translate into action with those who are in need; otherwise, people will not take our faith walk with God seriously.

Do you remember the World Heavyweight Champion boxer Muhammad Ali? Muhammad Ali was well known for his athletic skills, but his popularity grew among boxing audiences because he liked to show off his verbal wit to his opponents and the media before and after matches. One of his most famous statements was, "Float like a butterfly, sting like a bee, but don't you mess with Muhammad Ali." Ali didn't just talk, he backed up everything he said in the boxing ring. He did not just talk about being the best at his sport, he put action behind his talk.

Some Christians "talk a lot of stuff" about being a Christian. They may even go to church often. However, **1 John 3:16-18** reveals that being a Christian requires more than lip-service; it demands action.

The first epistle of John is generally divided into three parts: God is light (**1:1–2:27**); God is love (**2:28–4:21**); and God is life (**5:1-21**). For John these elements reveal the essence of who God is and how God acts in humanity as light, love, and life. God is action. God does not just say that God loves humanity; God shows it. Just as God remains active in humanity, those who have professed their love for God should also be instruments of this love by sharing God's love with others. Action is essential to love.

When a parent punishes a child, tells a child that he or she may not go to a movie, or refuses to give the child something that he or she wants, the angry child might say to the parent, "You don't love me." However, we know that, even during these fits of anger, parents really do love their children; because parents provide them with clothing, food, companionship, direction, and, yes, even a lot of other stuff that they want but do not really need. Parents keep taking care of their children, even though at times the children are disrespectful, make mistakes, and do not always meet their expectations. That's love. Parents do things for us, not to earn our love, but *because* they love us.

Someone can say a million times, "I love you," but never show it. If Muhammad Ali's opponents had consistently knocked him out in the first round after he had gone on and on about how he was going to do this and that, everyone would have thought that he was a joke. John wanted to emphasize to his Christian audience—and to today's Christians—that our talk of love for God should translate into action with those who are in need. Regardless of our intentions, without action, the words would carry no credibility.

For John, love for God meant love and service to humanity, especially the needy. How can you say that you are a Christian and ignore the homeless, the poor, the sick, the imprisoned, and others who have limited resources? How can Christian teenagers, who are dependent in many ways on their parents, turn their love for God into action? How can a needy person help someone else in need? Let's find out.

Tending	A/B	The Church in Action — or — From Talk to Action	Sending
Review Noticing God in Our Week Preview			Reflection Our Offering to God Blessing

Tending

(10–20 minutes) **Supplies:** *large, white candle; candleholder; matches*

❑ As the youth arrive, welcome them. Light the candle, and invite the youth into this sacred space and time. Begin the "Tending to God and One Another" conversation:
- Where were they aware of God in their week or in the world?
- What "highs" (good things) and what "lows" (rough things) did they experience during the week?
- What prayer requests do they have—either for themselves or on behalf of someone else?

❑ Ask the youth about their SMART goal. If they tried to live out their "offering to God" last week, how did it go? Encourage them in their discipleship efforts.

❑ Offer a prayer of thanksgiving for God's presence in the week and in the class. Lift up the group's highs and lows and prayer requests. Pray for God's guidance in this time together and along the journey.

❑ Take a few minutes to recall the previous week's word (*love*) and lesson. Invite those who were present to contribute to the review. Transition to the lesson (next page) by referring to today's word: *action*.

Sending

(5–10 minutes) **Supplies:** *paper or notecards, pens or pencils; candy or something else sweet for everyone*

❑ Ask the students to reflect silently on the lesson. What insights did they gain? What opportunities do they see to show God's love through their actions on behalf of people in need? Invite volunteers to offer some examples.

❑ As they are ready, have students write a SMART goal (**S**pecific, **M**easurable, **A**chievable, **R**evealed, and **T**ime limited). Remind them that living SMART is their offering to God for the coming week. Some of the activities in today's lesson should have stimulated possible ways.

❑ Send the group forth with a blessing of your choosing or say:

Go, with your eyes wide open. May you see the needy around you. May you see the gifts God has given you. May you show God's love in action! Go in peace.

Midweek Checklist

❑ Connect with youth.
❑ Inform parents.
❑ Look over supplies and preparation for Option A.

Sample SMART Goal

This week *(time-limited)* **I will identify one way to put God's love into action** *(measurable)* **and do it** *(specific, achievable and, we trust, revealed to the individual)*.

The Church in Action

Be-A

Supplies
• Imagination!

(15–20 minutes)

Have the youth work in groups of at least three to "Be-A (*something*)." Each group is to decide on an object (or animal) they want to be. They need also to decide how they will present the object (or animal) to the others. Encourage them to use sounds, motion, and other effects with their bodies. Give them time to organize. After a few minutes, have the groups come together to give their demonstrations while the others guess what they are. Ask:

• Was it possible to represent the object (or animal) without doing something?
• What was the purpose of the object? What actions showed that purpose?

Be a Christian

Supplies
• Bibles (in various versions)
• Bookzines
• Pens or pencils
• Sticky notes or slips of paper and tape
• Markers
• Markerboard or large sheet of paper

(15–20 minutes)

Have the youth find **1 John 3:16-18** and follow along in their Bibles as a volunteer reads the verses aloud. If possible, have volunteers read from different versions of the text, including *The Message,* which is printed on page 40 of the bookzine. Then have the youth discuss the meaning of the text, based on the readings from the various versions.

Christianity is more than a state of being (noun); it also requires an action (verb). Have the youth work individually as they do the exercise "Be a Christian" (bookzine, page 41). Read the instructions aloud and help them clarify "resources and attributes"; come up with additional examples, if possible, before they begin the task.

After a few minutes of individual time, have the youth work together to make a list of people they identified as needy. (Caution the group about using persons' names.) Have the class choose from the list one need to discuss further. Have the youth refer to their individual lists of their own resources and attributes and select one or two that would contribute to helping with this need. Have everyone write his or her contribution on a slip of paper or a sticky note and put it by the chosen need. Read aloud the resources and attitudes the youth have identified. Then ask:

• What does seeing all of our resources and attributes just within this classroom tell you? (*If we put all of these into action, we'd make a difference with this need.*)
• What if we took away half of those resources? What if only a few of you really turned your words into action? What difference would that make? (*Some vital resources could be missing; having more people working together to address a need is usually more effective—and more fun.*)
• What do we have here and around the world to help us address such needs? (*the church; the body of Christ with different gifts to put into action*)
• How does the Be a Christian exercise relate to the Be-A activity?
• Does a person love to be a Christian or do Christians love because they are Christian? What is the difference?
• Which comes first—love or action? [*Challenge the youth to make the case both ways.*]

From Talk to Action

Sacrificial Love

(15–20 minutes)

Have the youth find **1 John 3:16-18** in their Bibles; refer them also to the translation on page 42 of the bookzine. Ask the youth to work alone or in pairs to write their responses to the Bible study questions on the same page. Then have the group come together to talk about their answers to the questions there:

- What is the source of love for Christians? (*God loving us enough to send Christ to die for our sins; Christ willingly sacrificing his life for us.*)
- What does the Scripture assume about persons who do not have God's love living with them? (*John assumes that such persons—even though they have plenty—would refuse to help someone in need.*)
- What does it mean to live sacrificially? How does having God's love residing in us enable us to give to the needy? (*God has given us so much—sometimes in material goods, but especially in joy and love—that we can focus on others, giving up from our resources or giving of our attributes in order to share God's love with those in need.*)

True Love

(15–20 minutes)

Note that John is not talking about just any kind of love; John refers to God's love. Direct the youth to "Four Kinds of Love" (bookzine, page 43).

Have the group discuss times in which someone has said to them, "I love you." They may also use examples from others they know or from TV or movies. Ask:

- Did you believe it when he or she said it?
- What made it believable?
- What were some actions that expressed the love?
- What were some things that were done or not done that said, "This person does not love me"?

Have the youth revisit **1 John 3:16-18.** Have students write on page 44 of the bookzine the ways that they measure the truth and sincerity of their love for others, others' love for them, God's love for them, and their love for God. In other words, in what ways has love gone from talk to action? After a few minutes, ask:

- What do you see in your answers? What do they have in common?
- What if your boyfriend or girlfriend says that you have to have sex (an action) with him or her to prove your talk about love? How does that fit or not fit with what you see so far in this lesson? Hint: What is the nature of love? (*Love acts for the good of the other—not for momentary pleasure for oneself. With the very real consequences of teen sex—possible pregnancy, AIDS and other diseases, emotional costs—anyone demanding someone to prove love with sex before marriage is not showing love in the first place.*)

Supplies
- Bibles
- Bookzines
- Pens or pencils

 *Optional Activities*

Supplies
- Bookzines
- Pens or pencils

Honesty

Take Away

G... ...th integrity, dealing honestly with God, ourselves, and o...

Scripture

De... ...(All who act dishonestly God abhors.)

Additional Background

Filled with a series of laws that often make no sense in our culture, the Book of Deuteronomy can be a tough read. For example, you may eat water creatures that have fins and scales; you may not eat water creatures that do not have fins and scales. (No shrimp or lobster for dinner tonight.) You have to forgive all debts every seven years. (Wouldn't that be nice?) Rebellious children can be stoned to death. (That's not good—even if we are tempted some days!)

However, other rules have stood the test of time; one of these is honesty. This passage in Deuteronomy uses the image of a scale. A pre-determined weight was placed on one side and the item to be sold was placed on the other. For example, if you were selling a pound of grain to someone, you would put a one-pound weight on one side of the scale. Then you would measure grain into the other side until the scale was balanced. However, cheating was possible by using a deliberately inaccurate weight, fifteen instead of sixteen ounces, for example.

> *Dishonest dealings result in anger and mistrust, two emotions that can tear apart a community and that do not reflect the desire of God.*

Deuteronomy warned people to be fair in their dealings. Don't carry two kinds of measures, it says. Just use one measure that is accurate. Why? Because all who act dishonestly "are abhorrent to the LORD your God" (**Deuteronomy 25:16**). Why would dishonesty be so repugnant to God? What's the big deal? To God, the community is a big deal. The laws of the Torah, from the Ten Commandments down through seemingly smaller rules, were most often in place for the protection of the community. These were God's people, chosen to live in community as a witness to God for all. Dishonest dealings result in anger and mistrust, two emotions that can tear apart a community and that do not reflect the desire of God.

Youth encounter dishonesty all of the time. Sometimes they see it in people who live hypocritically, who tell the youth to live one way and then act otherwise. Sometimes they see it in the cheating that takes place at their school or at work. Studies have shown that significant numbers of youth believe that cheating is appropriate.

Talking about honesty is easier than living it. Tempting situations appear all of the time. Do you give change back to the sales clerk who gave you too much? Do you copy someone else's homework because you were helping someone else in trouble and didn't have time to study? Where do you draw the line?

> *Living honestly will mean that at times youth will be required to go against the people and conventional social expectations around them.*

Living honestly will mean that at times youth will be required to go against the people and conventional social expectations around them. Youth need to believe that ultimately honesty is best, even if the only payoff they experience is knowing that they did what is right in God's eyes.

A word of caution: Teens don't always know the difference between honesty and brutal honesty. They sometimes say things that, although true, are intended to be hurtful. One helpful criterion is to ask: Is my behavior helpful or hurtful?

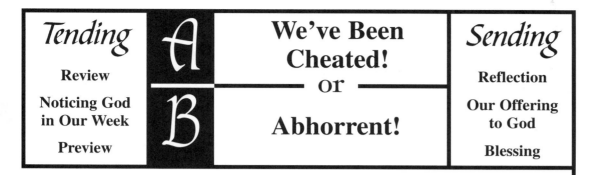

Tending		We've Been Cheated!	Sending
Review	**A**	or	Reflection
Noticing God in Our Week	**B**	Abhorrent!	Our Offering to God
Preview			Blessing

Tending

(10–20 minutes) **Supplies:** *large, white candle; candleholder; matches*

❏ As the youth arrive, welcome them. Light the candle, and invite the youth into this sacred space and time. Begin the "Tending to God and One Another" conversation:
- • Where were they aware of God in their week or in the world?
- • What "highs" (good things) and what "lows" (rough things) did they experience during the week?
- • What prayer requests do they have—either for themselves or on behalf of someone else?

❏ Ask the youth about their SMART goal. If they tried to live out their "offering to God" last week, how did it go? Encourage them in their discipleship efforts.

❏ Offer a prayer of thanksgiving for God's presence in the week and in the class. Lift up the group's highs and lows and prayer requests. Pray for God's guidance in this time together and along the journey.

❏ Take a few minutes to recall the previous week's word (*action*) and lesson. Invite those who were present to contribute to the review. Transition to the lesson (next page) by referring to today's word: *honesty*.

Sending

(5–10 minutes) **Supplies:** *paper or notecards, pens or pencils*

❏ Ask the youth to reflect silently on the lesson. What did they discover about honesty? Where are they planning to be honest in their relationships? Where do they need help?

❏ As they are ready, have the youth write a SMART goal (**S**pecific, **M**easurable, **A**chievable, **R**evealed, and **T**ime limited). Remind them that living SMART is their offering to God for the coming week.

❏ Send the group forth with the following blessing or another one of your choosing:

> God calls us to give full measure in all of our dealings. May you be honest in all that you do. Go in peace.

Midweek Checklist

❏ Connect with youth.
❏ Inform parents.
❏ Look over supplies for Option A.

Sample SMART Goal

This week (*time limited*) **I will be honest with my parents every day** (*measurable*) **when I tell them where I will be** (*specific, achievable, and, we trust, revealed to the individual*).

We've Been Cheated!

Building Blocks

(15–20 minutes)

Divide the youth into teams of four or five. Aim for an even number of groups. Give a set of the first instructions to half of the groups. Give the second set to the other teams. Don't let on that the instructions are different. Allow time for the teams to complete their structures. When the teams are finished, gather the groups; ask:

- How hard was it to build your structures?
- Did everyone follow the same rules? What were your instructions?
- How did you feel about having different rules applied?
- Sometimes different rules or measures are imposed in a situation where one would expect them to be the same. That treatment is referred to as a "double standard." Where in life have you encountered or heard of a double standard?
- Do you think that double standards are dishonest? Why, or why not?
- On a scale of *1* to *10,* how important do you think it is to be honest?
- Generally, how do people feel who have been cheated by a double standard or other dishonest practice? What consequences might occur because of the dishonesty?

What the Bible Says

(15–20 minutes)

Have the youth look up and read **Deuteronomy 25:13-16.** Explain that in biblical times, dishonest merchants would use different weights to measure such things as grain. For example, someone might order 5 pounds of grain, but the weights actually measured only 4.75 pounds, cheating the customer of a quarter pound, which would be hard to notice. Have the youth work in pairs or small groups to respond to the questions on page 48 of the bookzine. Then talk as a class about their answers and paraphrases.

Explain that the Book of Proverbs, in the Old Testament, contains a whole series of one-liners about living a good life. Some sound funny to us, and others are very familiar. **Proverbs 24:26** talks about honesty. The *New Revised Standard Version of the Bible* says that an honest answer is like "a kiss on the lips." *The Message* translates the verse to say "An honest answer is like a warm hug."

Divide the youth into teams of three. Have them follow the instructions in "Make a Proverb" (bookzine, page 47) as they create their own proverbs. When everyone has finished, bring the groups together for reporting. Ask:

- What are you saying about honesty?
- What is the hardest part about being honest?
- Is it ever wrong to be honest? Is it ever right to have a double standard?
- Why, do you think, does the Bible put such a heavy emphasis on honesty? on community? (*Dishonesty disrupts trust and affects the way a community functions.*)
- As a Christian, where in your life and relationships do you see the need for honesty? (This question could simply be for personal reflection.)

Supplies and Preparation
- Scrap pieces of 2-by-4 boards
- Tools
- Printed sets of instructions from the CD
- Ahead of time, cut 2x4's into 4-, 6-, and 8-inch lengths. Carpenters often have scraps of wood that you can use. You will need enough pieces for groups of four or five youth to build structures two feet high. The groups need identical sets of wood blocks.

Building Blocks Instruction Sheet

Optional Activities

Supplies
- Bibles
- Bookzines
- Pens or pencils

Abhorrent!

B

Two Truths and a Lie

(10–15 minutes)

Supplies
• Bookzines
• Pens or pencils

Give the youth two minutes to think of two truths about themselves and one lie. Then one at a time, they will tell their truths and lie to the rest of the group. Group members will try to determine which is the lie. For example: I was born in New York state. I like death-by-chocolate ice cream. I sang with a rock star. (*I was born in New York. I don't like death-by-chocolate ice cream. I sang with a rock star along with 3,000 other people in the auditorium.*)

If your class is large, work in smaller groups. Afterward, ask:

• What did you find out about one another?
• How easy was it to pick out the lie?
• On a scale of one to ten, how important is it to be honest?
• What is the connection between honesty and cheating?

Direct the youth to complete "Cheating—What Do You Think?" (bookzine, page 45). After they first work alone to fill in their response, have the youth review their responses in pairs. Together, they will develop a new set of responses. (They must agree on their answers.) Then come together and see whether the whole class can agree on a response to each situation. Then ask:

• What are we saying about cheating? about honesty?

What the Bible Says

(15–20 minutes)

Supplies
• Bibles
• Bookzine
• Pens or pencils

Have the youth look up and read **Deuteronomy 25:13-16.** Explain how cheating someone was possible by deliberately using inaccurate weights. Ask:

• If you had lived during that time, how would you feel if you had discovered that someone had cheated you in this way?
• What effect, do you think, that kind of cheating would have on the people who have been cheated? on the other people around them?
• In your experience, how has cheating or dishonesty affected people—including the cheater, the victim, and the community or other people in the group? Tell some stories.
• On a scale of *1* to *10,* how strongly does God dislike dishonesty? Why, do you think, would God's reaction to dishonesty be so strong?

Have the youth work in groups of two or three to rewrite the Scripture in their own words, using examples from their own world. (See page 48 of the bookzine.) Then gather the groups together to listen to their paraphrases.

Hospitality

Take Away

As Christians, we are to extend hospitality, inviting strangers in and attending to their needs, making them welcome in our space.

Scripture

Hebrews 13:1-2 (Do not neglect hospitality.)

Additional Background

Susan met the new intern at the door, greeting her warmly. Jennifer was to be with the team for ten weeks. Before she came, we had sent her leads for possible housing since she was from another state. She found a place with one of Susan's friends. Her first day we brought Jennifer to her office, which three days earlier had only had leftovers from the previous occupant. However, Sheila and Keely had transformed it to not only a functional space, but also a fun place with playful frogs and a laughing horse on the walls. Members of the team gathered to welcome Jennifer; we presented her with a basket of brochures of fun things to do in town, practical stuff (a map, a notebook, and a pen), and the all-important chocolate bars! As Christians, our team was doing what has become natural to us—showing hospitality, welcoming the stranger.

Following God's way often results in surprise blessings.

In biblical tradition, hospitality is an act of faithfulness. Before the days of motels and restaurants, a traveler's very survival depended upon the hospitality of those who welcomed, fed, and gave shelter to people they did not know and would likely never see again. Numerous stories in the Bible are indications of the importance of this act of hospitality.

Perhaps the most famous is **Genesis 18:1-15.** In this story Abraham saw three strangers. He literally "ran from the tent entrance to meet them" and invited them to a meal, prepared with the best of ingredients. Abraham was following the custom of hospitality, but he was to discover that surprises were in it for him. The "three men" told of the fulfillment of the covenant: Sarah would have a son within the next year. The nearly ninety-year-old Sarah laughed. But the laugh was joyfully on her. Indeed, Isaac was born as foretold. The "three men" were at the very least angels (messengers of God) and quite likely even the triune Lord in the flesh (see verses 1 and 13).

For the early Christians who heard **Hebrews 13:2,** the reference to "some have entertained angels without knowing it" would have rung true as they recalled this treasured story of the faith. Following God's way often results in surprise blessings.

The church needs to provide youth with an example of an alternative to the hostile environs in which they must also function.

What about youth? With exclusion and meanness a very real part of their experience, how do we help them include and treat others as special? How do we give them the courage to be welcoming when they know that action may well result in their being unwelcome in a certain group? How do we teach them to look beyond themselves to see the potential for turning strangers into friends, to canceling out hostility with hospitality?

The church needs to provide youth with an example of an alternative to the hostile environs in which they must also function. So, one starting point is an assessment of your church, your youth group, your Sunday school class. How well is the community of faith welcoming youth and others? What students see and experience will have an even greater impact than what we say. But this lesson, coupled with positive experience, can teach youth to practice hospitality as followers of God's way.

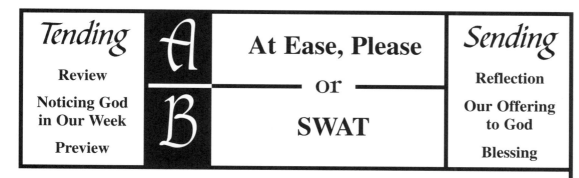

Tending	A B	At Ease, Please or SWAT	Sending
Review Noticing God in Our Week Preview			Reflection Our Offering to God Blessing

Tending

(10–20 minutes) **Supplies:** *large, white candle; candleholder; matches*

❑ As the youth arrive, welcome them. Light the candle, and invite the youth into this sacred space and time. Begin the "Tending to God and One Another" conversation:
   • Where were they aware of God in their week or in the world?
   • What "highs" (good things) and what "lows" (rough things) did they experience during the week?
   • What prayer requests do they have—either for themselves or on behalf of someone else?

❑ Ask the youth about their SMART goal. If they tried to live out their "offering to God" last week, how did it go? Encourage them in their discipleship efforts.

❑ Offer a prayer of thanksgiving for God's presence in the week and in the class. Lift up the group's highs and lows and prayer requests. Pray for God's guidance in this time together and along the journey.

❑ Take a few minutes to recall the previous week's word (*honesty*) and lesson. Invite those who were present to contribute to the review. Transition to the lesson (next page) by referring to today's word: *hospitality*.

Sending

(5–10 minutes) **Supplies:** *paper or notecards, pens or pencils*

❑ Offer a period of silence so that students have an opportunity to reflect on the session. Ask them to consider any new insights about hospitality, offering kindness to strangers, or other ideas brought forth in discussion. Invite volunteers to offer their thoughts.

❑ As they are ready, have the students write a SMART goal (**S**pecific, **M**easurable, **A**chievable, **R**evealed, and **T**ime limited). Encourage them to think of something specific to do for a particular person or in a situation of which they are currently a part. The ideas they generated in the session are good starting points.

❑ Close with a blessing of your choosing or this one based on **Hebrews 13:2:**

   "Do not neglect to show hospitality to strangers, for by doing that some have entertained angels without knowing it." May you grow in your desire to welcome others, and may you experience God's surprise blessings because you have been faithful. Go in peace.

Midweek Checklist

❑ Connect with youth.
❑ Inform parents.
❑ Have on hand *Veracity Video Vignettes, Volume 3,* for Option B.

Sample SMART Goal

This week at school (*time limited*) **I will talk with one person I don't know** (*measurable*) **and invite him or her to eat lunch with my circle of friends** (*specific, achievable and, we trust, revealed to the individual*)**.**

At Ease, Please

What Is Hospitality?

Supplies
• Bookzines
• Pens or pencils
• Paper

(20–25 minutes)

Direct the youth to **Hebrews 13:1-2,** printed on page 50 of the bookzine. Have a volunteer read it aloud, plus the definition of *hospitality* on that same page. Ask youth for some examples of showing hospitality—or of being inhospitable. After a few illustrations, invite volunteers to put into their own words what hospitality is.

Divide the youth into smaller teams. Refer them to "Let's Do It!" (bookzine, page 51). Assign to the different teams one of the tasks. You may give multiple teams the same task if necessary. The teams are to use the questions with the task to figure out ways to show hospitality and will also make a presentation to the whole group.

After a few minutes, call for the presentations. The teams may simply give a report of what they talked about and decided or they may do a demonstration of what they think would show hospitality or a skit of the opposite of hospitality, for example.

Optional Activities

After each presentation, ask questions for clarification and be sure to affirm their work. After all of the teams finish, ask:

• What difference does showing hospitality make in church? at school? in our world?
• How do people feel when they have been noticed in positive ways? How does that contribute to the overall good?
• What might people feel when they are ignored or actively shunned? How might those feelings affect others? (*School violence may be one example.*)
• What are some of the things that make it hard to be hospitable? Why? (*fear of the unknown, fear of being rejected, fear of what other people will think; being self-centered, not being aware of others, not knowing what do or how to do it*)
• What would help us and others get past those barriers and be more hospitable? (*having friends who also practice hospitality and who are supportive of us, seeing others being hospitable, knowing that as Christians we are to welcome and care for others, trusting God to help us*)

Let's Do It!

Supplies
• Bookzines
• Pens or pencils

(5–10 minutes)

Refer the group to "We Feel Awkward . . ." (bookzine, page 53). Have a volunteer read it aloud. Invite reactions and ideas from the group. Point out that this group figured out a way to help themselves get past some of the barriers.

Invite the group to brainstormed ways in addition to the others they've already talked about to show hospitality. Assure the group that even a small act of hospitality is a place to start as they begin this spiritual practice.

SWAT

What's Wrong Here?

(10–15 minutes)

Show "SWAT," the interview with the SWAT members. Ask the youth to work in threes to quickly identify five things wrong with the SWAT group's "hospitality." Then have the trios tell one thing at a time and briefly discuss each until you have listed all of the things the youth saw as not hospitable. Play the vignette again, if you'd like, and allow the youth to add to the list if they have new ideas.

Here are some questions to use if the youth need any prompting:

- What was the stated purpose of the SWAT team? How did members treat one another? How did they treat outsiders?
- Who showed more hospitality: Michael Frontman or the SWAT members?
- Which Scripture was used in the SWAT contract? Why do you think it was used?
- How would you set up a group dedicated to showing hospitality to others? Is hospitality a program or an attitude? a group or an individual responsibility? or both?

Supplies
- Bibles
- *Veracity Video Vignettes, Volume 3,* ("SWAT")
- DVD player and TV
- Bookzines
- Pens or pencils
- Markerboard or large sheets of paper
- Markers

What's Right?

(10–15 minutes)

Ask a volunteer to read aloud **Hebrews 13:1-2,** printed on page 50 of the bookzine. Ask another to read aloud the definitions on that same page. Invite volunteers to put in their own words what the passage is saying.

Then ask the youth for examples of showing hospitality. Encourage them to contrast the positive examples with the negative they discussed about the SWAT interview. Together make another list of ways to show hospitality.

Direct the youth to "Stranger or Not?" (bookzine, page 52). Have the youth first work individually to determine who qualifies as "a stranger," in their experience. When they have completed the page, read the list in the bookzine aloud and ask for a show of hands to indicate how many youth identified each entry as a stranger. Note any listings that the youth disagreed on. After going over the list, ask for a show of hands of how many youth classified more than half as strangers? More than three-quarters? Then ask:

- What were your criteria for classifying someone as a stranger? [*Discuss why some students marked someone as a stranger and others did not. What made a difference?*]
- If you knew people personally in a specific category, did that factor affect your answers? How? [*Point out that one way we turn strangers into no-longer-strangers is by getting to know them, which often begins with an act of hospitality on our part.*]

Give the youth a moment to look over the three lists they have created. Challenge them to choose at least one stranger to whom they will show hospitality as the focus of their SMART goal. Assure the youth that hospitality is an important part of our discipleship.

Supplies
- Bookzines
- Pens or pencils
- Markerboard or large sheets of paper
- Markers

Brokenness

God can take the brokenness in our life and create something new and whole.

Psalm 51:16-17 (I can come to God with my brokenness.)

Additional Background

We are a consumer society. We take our "stuff," use and misuse it, and then wonder why it doesn't last. When it breaks or stops working, we throw it aside. Too often, fixing broken things requires too much time or too much energy; frankly, buying a new one is often cheaper—and certainly more fun. Resale shops and charity-based stores are filled with castoffs that are beautiful, high quality, and useable. We just nicked it, it went out of style, or we got tired of it. So in our constant search for the perfect life filled with the perfect stuff, we toss it, throw it away. After all, we work hard for our money. We should be able to treat ourselves and maintain a standard of living that we deserve. We shouldn't have to live with broken and cracked things.

Unfortunately, we take that rationale to heart with the other "things" in our lives too. You see, our lives have intangible things that threaten to break and crack us. Dead-end relationships, substance abuse, poverty, cancer, hunger—all of these things threaten to bankrupt us spiritually. They cause us to question ourselves; question our relationships; and yes, even question God. We point fingers, cast blame, and get angry all in an attempt to make sense of what is happening to us. When all is said and done, though, we are still in pain, broken. And when that happens, we are left to wonder how we can be "fixed." How can we ever return to normal (whatever that is)? Will we ever be the same? What can we do to get better?

> *When we finally realize that we have no control over our own lives, we can turn to God.*

The truth is, we can do *nothing* on our own to be truly fixed. Certainly, we can read self-help books or watch Dr. Phil and Oprah for suggestions to work toward an understanding of what is happening in our own life or even take on new hobbies to simply forget. But when we're at the very bottom, when we find no motivation to search for a solution, no hope that there even is a solution, when we finally realize that we have no control over our own lives, we can turn to God. At that point, God can step in, take our brokenness, and reshape us into something beautiful—never the same, never back to the original self, but reformed to a better self, a new creation.

God, the master potter, takes the piece of clay that is you, fallen apart, shattered perhaps, seemingly of no use to you or to anyone else. God reworks the clay, kneading it, pounding it, and then lovingly and painstakingly creating a new you, a better you, a stronger you. The brokenness that threatens to overtake you and consume you, God can use to make you new and whole in a different way.

> *God can use the brokenness that threatens to overtake you and consume you to make you new and whole in a different way.*

Aren't we blessed to know that God doesn't buy in to that "consumer society" mentality? Isn't it reassuring to know that God cares so much about each one of us that God takes our brokenness and pieces it back together into something even better? Despite our knicks, cracks, and imperfections, God loves us as perfectly. We are not to be cast aside or thrown away. We are lovingly protected and perfected by our Creator. What a blessing!

Tending	A B	Humpty Dumpty Can't or That Broken Place	Sending
Review Noticing God in Our Week Preview			Reflection Our Offering to God Blessing

Tending

(10–20 minutes) **Supplies:** *large, white candle; candleholder; matches*

❏ As the youth arrive, welcome them. Light the candle, and invite the youth into this sacred space and time. Begin the "Tending to God and One Another" conversation:
- Where were they aware of God in their week or in the world?
- What "highs" (good things) and what "lows" (rough things) did they experience during the week?
- What prayer requests do they have—either for themselves or on behalf of someone else?

❏ Ask the youth about their SMART goal. If they tried to live out their "offering to God" last week, how did it go? Encourage them in their discipleship efforts.

❏ Offer a prayer of thanksgiving for God's presence in the week and in the class. Lift up the group's highs and lows and prayer requests. Pray for God's guidance in this time together and along the journey.

❏ Take a few minutes to recall the previous week's word (*hospitality*) and lesson. Invite those who were present to contribute to the review. Transition to the lesson (next page) by referring to today's word: *brokenness.*

Sending

(5–10 minutes) **Supplies:** *paper or notecards, pens or pencils (Optional: enough pieces of broken glass or pottery for each youth to have one [Be sure to make sure that none of them have sharp edges.])*

❏ Refer the youth to page 56 in the bookzine. Allow them time to reflect silently on the lesson. What did they discover about brokenness? What has become clear to them? How have they experienced or seen brokenness in their lives or in the lives of others? After a few minutes invite volunteers to offer their thoughts.

❏ As they are ready, have the students write a SMART goal (**S**pecific, **M**easurable, **A**chievable, **R**evealed, and **T**ime limited). Remind them that living SMART is their offering to God for the coming week.

❏ If you have pieces of broken pottery or glass, give one to each student as a reminder. Send the class forth with the following blessing or another one of your choosing:

> In your brokenness, may you turn to the One who can truly heal and make you whole again. Go with the assurance of God's love and power. Go in peace.

Midweek Checklist

❏ Connect with youth.
❏ Inform parents.
❏ Look over supplies and preparation for both options.

Sample SMART Goal

This week (*time limited*) **I will identify one place** (*measurable*) **in my life or in the lives of those around me where there is brokenness. I will pray each day for God to bring healing** (*specific, achievable, and, we trust, revealed to the individual*).

Humpty Dumpty Can't

Broken Shells

(20–25 minutes)

Have each youth use a permanent marker to write his or her name on a zippered bag. Then have the youth carefully break an egg (or two) into the bag, and to save his or her own shells. Let the youth add their choice of omelet ingredients to the bag and zip the bag closed. Have the youth squeeze the bag until the contents are mixed well. Drop the bags into boiling water for about 15 minutes. While the omelets cook, challenge the youth to put their egg shells back together. Give a prize for the first person who comes closest to getting his or her egg back together. Allow about 3 minutes.

Remove the omelets from the water, have the youth empty their bag onto a paper plate. While the class enjoys the meal, point out that, sometimes when we break things, they can be easily put together. But some things seem beyond repair. Ask:

• Have you ever broken something you really cared about? Was it able to be fixed?
• Have you ever tried to hide something you had broken? Why, or why not?
• What are some "things" that you know, if broken, can't be easily fixed? (*trust, relationships, commitments, vows*)

Broken Spirits

(10–15 minutes)

Refer the youth to the two versions of **Psalm 51:15-17,** on the page 54 of the bookzine. Have volunteers read aloud first from the NRSV and then from *The Message*. Ask:

• What does God *not* want from us?
• What does it mean to just "go through the motions"?
• What is acceptable to God, according to these versions of the Scripture passage?
• What does it mean to have a broken and contrite heart? a broken spirit? How is that like a heart shattered ready for love?
• What do we need to give up? (*pride in ourselves, trying to be the one in control*)
• What, do you think, is the psalmist trying to say about us? about God? about our relationship with God?

Say, "God knows that many of us try to control our own lives. As humans, we want to be in charge or in control of who we are. Our pride in ourselves replaces our love for God. When we try to control our own lives, we turn our back on God; and when we do that, we often find ourselves making bad choices and even falling apart. We become like those egg shells—broken and shattered—and we don't have the ability to put the pieces back together. Only God, the great physician, knows how to mend our brokenness. Only God can put us back together again."

Hold up an egg or egg shell. Point out that an egg is little good to us in its original state. Its usefulness and value begin when it is broken open. That's how we are—only useful and useable by God when we can let go of our shell of pride and control and open ourselves to God to heal, to guide, to use.

Supplies and Preparation
• Hot plates or access to a kitchen stovetop
• 1 or 2 raw eggs for each youth
• Soap and water or wet-wipes
• Ingredients for omelets, such as: grated cheese, chopped tomatoes, mushrooms, green peppers, onions
• Zippered food storage bag for each youth
• Permanent marker
• Paper plates, forks, napkins
• Prize for the winner

Teacher Tip
Some egg shells have been found to carry salmonella. Be sure to have everyone wash their hands after touching the eggs.

Supplies
• Bookzines

That Broken Place

"Fix You"

(15–20 minutes)

Play the song "Fix You" or read aloud the lyrics. Direct the youth to "That Broken Place" (bookzine, page 55). Give them about ten minutes to write. As an alternative, have pairs or trios of youth talk quietly about the bookzine activity. (Some youth will do better with the introspection of writing; others will be better able to identify feelings if they can think aloud with one or two trusted friends.) Assure the youth this activity is for them alone, not for the group.

Bring the group back together, then ask:

* What does this song say will "guide you home and ignite your bones"? (*lights*)
* Who is our light? (*God/Christ*)

Shattered

(15–20 minutes)

Direct the youth to **Psalm 51:16-17,** on the page 54 of the bookzine. Give the youth some background: Sacrificing was part of the expected way of worshiping God, including atoning for (asking forgiveness for) sins. Ask two volunteers to read the two translations. Have them each read both versions of verse 16 before they read verse 17.

Divide the youth into at least two groups. Assign half of the groups verse 16 and half verse 17. Each group is to look at both versions of the verse and determine what they think the psalmist means. Then they are to connect with a group that has the other verse. Both groups tell the other what it has determined. Then both groups work together to decide what **Psalm 51:16-17** means. Then invite volunteers to articulate the meaning of the passage. Ask follow-up questions as needed.

Hold up some pottery. Invite the youth to describe what happens on a potter's wheel.

Say: "When a potter makes something from a piece of clay, it doesn't always come out perfectly the first time. The potter positions a ball of clay on the wheel. As the wheel spins, the potter gently and delicately uses his or her hands to form the pitcher, bowl, vase, or other item. The slightest wrong touch can cause the clay to collapse, to lose its shape, to fall over, or even fly off the wheel. When that happens, the potter takes the clay, mashes it down, reworks it by kneading and prodding it, and then starts over."

Point out the similarity with our Master Potter: Even the slightest touch of something bad can cause us to collapse, to crumble. We encounter things that make us stumble and fall. But when we are broken, our loving potter gently and delicately picks up the pieces of our lives, reworks us by filling our hearts with love and grace, and then starts reshaping us into an even more beautiful creation. The pain and hurt of our brokenness may linger, but it is steadily and most assuredly overridden by a sense of being held in God's hands. When we allow ourselves the freedom to let God reshape us and not try to fix ourselves, the result is much more beautiful than we can ever have imagined.

Supplies
* "Fix You," by Coldplay (*Fix You*) and a CD or MP3 Player (Alternative: Play "Fix You" on the website *www.Deezer.com*.)
* Optional: Find the lyrics to "Fix You" online.

 *Optional Activities*

Supplies
* Bookzines
* Pens or pencils
* Piece of pottery (optional)

Hardship

The assurance of God's presence with us during difficult times and God's ability to make a bad situation good enable us to endure hardship.

Genesis 41:46-52 (God has made me forget all my hardship.)

Additional Background

Although Joseph could have blamed God for all of his hardships, he blessed God for delivering him.

Living as a Christian does not necessarily mean that our lives will be easy. We all have experienced hard times, encountered problems, faced loss, experienced sadness, been rejected. We cannot escape hardship; however, we can choose how we will respond to it.

In our verses, we witness the testimony of a man who endured many hardships. However, Joseph named his sons Manasseh ("For . . . God has made me forget all my hardship and all my father's house") and Ephraim ("For God has made me fruitful in the land of my misfortunes"). Rejected, sold into slavery, lied about, and imprisoned, Joseph could have blamed God for all of his hardships. However, in spite of his difficult situations, he blessed God for delivering him safely, easing the emotional hurt, and enabling him to be a prosperous man and a contributor to the welfare of others.

Jacob, Joseph's father, had always favored him, which did not go unnoticed by Jacob's other sons. Anger and jealousy erupted and grew into hate through a series of events detailed in **Genesis 37:2-11:1**). Joseph "brought a bad report of [the brothers] to their father"; 2) Jacob gave Joseph a special robe (traditionally called the "coat of many colors"); and 3) Joseph had a series of dreams, which he interpreted to his brothers as being about them "bowing down" to him. Their hatred for Joseph grew to the extent that they plotted to murder their brother. Instead of carrying out the killing, though, they sold Joseph into slavery. Then he was taken to Egypt, where he was again sold, this time to Potiphar, a high-ranking Egyptian. **Genesis 39:3-4** says:

> His master [Potiphar] saw that the LORD was with [Joseph], and that the LORD caused all that he did to prosper in his hands. So Joseph found favor in [Potiphar's] sight and attended him; [Potiphar] made [Joseph] overseer of his house and put him in charge of all that he had.

If we continue to trust in God, as Joseph did, we shall experience difficult situations turned into amazing opportunities to grow in God's grace.

But while Potiphar trusted Joseph, Potiphar's wife lusted for handsome, young Joseph. When Joseph refused her advances, she accused him of rape; and Joseph went to jail.

Joseph really had some tough times. Hardship is not always a result of our misconduct. Sometimes "stuff" just happens. Sometimes hardship comes from the anger and evil in others, which may be provoked by something good (such as the special favor shown to Joseph).

When hardships happen like this, the temptation is to give up on God and lose faith. However, if we continue to trust in God as Joseph did, we shall experience difficult situations turned into amazing opportunities to grow in God's grace. The assurance of God's presence with us during difficult times and God's ability to make a bad situation good enable us to endure hardship.

Tending	A/B	It's Inevitable, But... — or — The Way Out Is Through	Sending
Review Noticing God in Our Week Preview			Reflection Our Offering to God Blessing

Tending

(10–20 minutes) **Supplies:** *large, white candle; candleholder; matches*

❑ As the youth arrive, welcome them. Light the candle, and invite the youth into this sacred space and time. Begin the "Tending to God and One Another" conversation:
  - Where were they aware of God in their week or in the world?
  - What "highs" (good things) and what "lows" (rough things) did they experience during the week?
  - What prayer requests do they have—either for themselves or on behalf of someone else?

❑ Ask the youth about their SMART goal. If they tried to live out their "offering to God" last week, how did it go? Encourage them in their discipleship efforts.

❑ Offer a prayer of thanksgiving for God's presence in the week and in the class. Lift up the group's highs and lows and prayer requests. Pray for God's guidance in this time together and along the journey.

❑ Take a few minutes to recall the previous week's word (*brokenness*) and lesson. Invite those who were present to contribute to the review. Transition to the lesson (next page) by referring to today's word: *hardship*.

Sending

(5–10 minutes) **Supplies:** *paper or notecards, pens or pencils*

❑ Give the youth some silence to reflect on the lesson. What did they discover about hardship? What new insights have they gained? Would any of them like to be added to your prayer list as they deal with hardship in their lives now? Invite volunteers to share their thoughts.

❑ As they are ready, have the students write a SMART goal (**S**pecific, **M**easurable, **A**chievable, **R**evealed, and **T**ime limited). Remind them that living SMART is their offering to God for the coming week.

❑ Send the group forth with a blessing of your choosing or say:

> In the midst of hardship, we are not alone. God is with us, comforting and guiding us. When we turn to God, we can trust God to see us through and bless us. Go in peace.

Midweek Checklist

❑ Connect with youth.
❑ Inform parents.
❑ Look over supplies and preparation for both options.

Sample SMART Goal

This week (*time-limited*) **I will focus on a hardship—past or present—in my life** (*specific*) **and look for at least three ways God is helping or has helped me through it** (*measurable, achievable, and, we trust, revealed to the individual*).

It's Inevitable, But . . .

From Crisis

(15–20 minutes)

Give each student a puzzle. Do not hand out the extra puzzle piece or tell the youth that some puzzles have a piece is missing. Offer a small reward to the youth who completes his or her puzzle first.

When someone completes the puzzle (of course, only those without a missing piece can do so), give him or her a small prize. After a few minutes, invite groups to talk about the activity. Ask:

- Who had a puzzle piece missing? How did you discover that it was gone?
- How did you feel about the fact that I (the teacher) intentionally withheld the piece?
- If you were able to complete the puzzle, what hardships did you experience? How did you handle them?
- If you weren't able to complete the puzzle, what hardships did you encounter? How did you handle them?
- For those who weren't able to complete the puzzle, are you still in crisis? Why?

To Crown

(15–20 minutes)

Point out that Christians often think of Joseph when discussing the subject of hardship. Have the youth find **Genesis 41:46-52** in their Bible. Have a volunteer read it aloud. Tell the youth that this event is near the end of Joseph's story; to get the full picture of Joseph's troubles, they need to do the Bible study on page 59 of the bookzine.

Divide the youth into small groups to do the Bible study. You may choose to divide up the assignment among the various groups. Each group is to record Joseph's hardships. At the end of the section, they are to look for God at work.

After a few minutes, discuss the exercise, clarifying points as needed. Then give the missing puzzle pieces to the youth who had not been able to complete their puzzle. Ask:

- How does it feel to have hardship while watching others going through life seemingly without problems? (*Joseph suffers as an innocent man, but he still trusts in God through hardship.*) [Draw in the different puzzle groups; and note that at the end of exercise, everyone was able to accomplish the goal.]
- How can we experience God's presence in the midst of hardship? (*Encourage the youth not to focus on the hardship but on the good things that are happening in their lives; help them learn to look for God at work during the hard places in life.*)
- Can we really forget all of our hardships? (*We do not forget them; we just do not constantly dwell on them so that they control our lives.*)
- What clues do you take from the story of Joseph for how to deal with the inevitable hardships you will encounter in life?

Hand out a small prize to each youth who didn't receive one before.

Supplies and Preparation
- Envelopes or food storage plastic bags
- Construction paper of various colors
- Scissors
- Small prizes (one for each youth)
- For each youth, cut one sheet of construction paper into no more than 16 "puzzle pieces." Do not simply cut the paper into squares; cut some wavy, some angular, and some jigsaw-like lines. Place the pieces for each puzzle into a bag or envelope. Remove one piece from half of the bags.

Teacher Tip
If your class is large, cut one puzzle for each for pair, trio, or other small group.

Supplies
- Bibles
- Bookzines
- Pens or pencils

The Way Out Is Through

Hard and Harder

(15–20 minutes)

Direct the youth to pages 58–59 of the bookzine. They are to create a storyboard or outline of Joseph's hardships. You may choose to assign sections of the activity and then put everything together later. Their storyboard may be simple sketches, even basic stick figures, to represent the events or a phrase or two on a sheet of paper. Have a space on the wall or on the floor or lay out the sheets of paper and put the story in sequence. Have the youth use the storyboard or outline to give the highlights of Joseph's experiences. Fill in any missing details. Then ask:

- How many years did Joseph have to endure this series of hardships? (*Genesis 37:2 says that Joseph was seventeen; Genesis 41:46 gives his age as thirty. Point out that hardships can last for many years.*)
- If you were in any of the situations that Joseph faced, how might you—or others you know—have responded? (*fear, anger, despair, seeking revenge*)
- What indications did Joseph have of God's continuing care for him during those years? (*The brothers didn't kill him. He prospered in Potiphar's house initially. He still had the gift of interpretation, which he knew was from God.*)

Deal With It?

(15–20 minutes)

Invite the youth to reflect on the hardships in their own lives or in the lives of persons they know or know about. Encourage them to write on page 60 of the bookzine. Assure them this writing is for them, not for sharing with the group.

After a few minutes, have a volunteer read aloud **Genesis 41:50-52.** Explain to them that Joseph is declaring that God enabled him to forget his hardships, and he is also thanking God for making a bad situation turn out to be a good one. Point out to the youth that when we do not address our problems in a healthy way, bad situations can turn into worse ones. Challenge the youth to come up with healthy ways to deal with hardship, based especially—but not exclusively—on Joseph's story.

You may choose to have the youth make a list on a markerboard or large sheet of paper. Or have the youth to work in small groups to make a list. Compile the ideas and send them out in the midweek communication to your youth. Here are some key points you may want to add or emphasize:

- Experiencing hardship does not mean that God does not love you or that you have done something wrong. Sometimes our hardships are of our own making.
- Hardship does not last forever. "This too shall pass."
- In our hardships, we need to turn *to* God rather than *away*. God is worthy of trust.
- We do not have a choice as to whether we will experience hardship, but we have a choice about how we respond to it.
- As members of the body of Christ, we can help one another through hardships.

Supplies
- Bibles
- Bookzines
- Pens and pencils
- Paper
- Markers and/or crayons
- Tape

Supplies
- Bibles
- Markerboard or large sheets of paper
- Markers
- Tape

Generosity

Biblical generosity comes from a loving heart, a willing spirit, and a cheerful attitude.

Deuteronomy 15:7-11 (Open your heart to the poor and needy.)

Additional Background

When natural disasters strike, we often see celebrities, worth millions of dollars, participating in benefit concerts and televised fundraisers to generate money for relief efforts. Others use their fame and fortune to attack societal plights such as world hunger, AIDS, and other worthy causes. While these contributions are certainly appreciated and much needed, they also challenge our notion of generosity. Isn't it easy to give away your money when you have a lot of it? Doesn't not having lots of money let the rest of us off?

Christians are called to generosity—selfless and sacrificial giving. The biblical notion of generosity encompasses freely giving from one's resources—however large or seemingly small. Certainly those gifts include monetary donations, but they also include intangible offerings. How willingly do you give your time, your service, your prayers? How generously do you listen and give care? Would you rather "throw money" at a problem than roll up your sleeves to do the hard work of making change?

Christians are called to generosity—selfless and sacrificial giving

And, says the Scripture, when a believer does give money (regardless of the dollar amount), it should be given cheerfully, willingly, and with love. Generosity is an attitude, not an amount. A generous giver glorifies God simply by meeting another's need with the love of Christ.

Deuteronomy 15:7-11 is best understood in context. It is in a section of the Law commanding the Israelites to forgive debts every seventh year. This provision is a beautiful foreshadowing of the grace of the gospel: Believers' debts (sins) are erased by the blood of Christ. God next addresses the motive of the mind and heart, reminding the people that although they are obligated to forgive, they must do so with the right attitude. God calls the people to a lifestyle of giving, addressing needs in the land and denying no one.

Regardless of the gift given, generosity is chiefly a state of the heart.

Meeting needs begins with knowing what those needs are. Many well-meaning Christians today elect, instead, to "hide their heads in the sand" or huddle together with other like-minded persons. Ignoring problems in your community will not fix them nor will it bring people the love of Christ. Jesus says:

> "You are the light of the world. A city built on a hill cannot be hid. No one after lighting a lamp puts it under the bushel basket, but on the lampstand, and it gives light to all in the house. In the same way, let your light shine before others, so that they may see your good works and give glory to your Father in heaven."—**Matthew 5:14-16**

We are called to give generously as we have been generously blessed by God. All sorts of needs exist among our neighbors. Money may be needed, but God also blesses your generous gifts of kind words, acts of service, and devoted prayers. Regardless of the gift given, generosity is chiefly a state of the heart.

Tending	A	Open Hands	Sending
Review Noticing God in Our Week Preview	**A** **B**	or **Who Answered the Call?**	Reflection Our Offering to God Blessing

Tending

(10–20 minutes) **Supplies:** *large, white candle; candleholder; matches*

❏ As the youth arrive, welcome them. Light the candle, and invite the youth into this sacred space and time. Begin the "Tending to God and One Another" conversation:
  - Where were they aware of God in their week or in the world?
  - What "highs" (good things) and what "lows" (rough things) did they experience during the week?
  - What prayer requests do they have—either for themselves or on behalf of someone else?

❏ Ask the youth about their SMART goal. If they tried to live out their "offering to God" last week, how did it go? Encourage them in their discipleship efforts.

❏ Offer a prayer of thanksgiving for God's presence in the week and in the class. Lift up the group's highs and lows and prayer requests. Pray for God's guidance in this time together and along the journey.

❏ Take a few minutes to recall the previous week's word (*hardship*) and lesson. Invite those who were present to contribute to the review. Transition to the lesson (next page) by referring to today's word: *generosity*.

Sending

(5–10 minutes) **Supplies:** *paper or notecards, pens or pencils*

❏ Ask the students to reflect in silence on the lesson. What did they discover about generosity? What has become clear to them? What things they were reminded of? What new things did they realize? Invite volunteers to share.

❏ As they are ready, have the students write a SMART goal (**S**pecific, **M**easurable, **A**chievable, **R**evealed, and **T**ime limited). Remind them that living SMART is their offering to God for the coming week.

❏ Send the group forth with a blessing of your choosing, or use this one based on **2 Corinthians 9:7-8.** Ask them to open their hands as they receive the blessing.

> Go forward with a generous heart and open hands, looking for ways to give yourself to the needs around you. What God commands you to do, God is faithful to equip you to do. The passage **2 Corinthians 9:7-8** says, "God loves a cheerful giver. And God is able to provide you with every blessing in abundance, so that by always having enough of everything, you may share abundantly in every good work." Go in peace.

Midweek Checklist

Sample SMART Goal

I will identify one need of a friend or family member (*measurable*). **Each day of this week** (*time limited*) **I will pray that I would meet that need with a generous spirit and act upon what the Holy Spirit reveals to me** (*specific, achievable and, we trust, revealed to the individua*l).

Open Hands

Budgeting the Funds

Supplies
• Bookzines
• Pens or pencils
• Calculators
  (optional)

(20–25 minutes)

Have the youth gather into pairs or trios. Refer them to the "Budget Worksheet" (bookzine, pages 66–69). Ask them to roleplay that they are in charge of allocating $750,000 of the state's funds among the seven state groups listed there. Teams should read about the groups and, based on the information, decide how to disperse the money.

Encourage the youth to think about the exercise in terms of their Christian convictions and what they already know about scriptural commands on giving and generosity. (The goal of the activity is not to see how well they can balance a budget, but it is to sharpen their decision-making skills. They will also better appreciate the various needs in their community. This activity may cause the youth to consider what it means to be generous.)

Once they are finished with the budget activity pages, the teams will report to the class the reasons for their decisions. Give the class permission to politely challenge any decisions they don't agree with. The youth should defend their decisions with reasonable explanations and examples. After all of the teams have presented, ask:

 Optional Activities

• What was hard about this exercise? What was easy?
• How did being a Christian influence your decisions?
• What if you could have known more about the persons involved (individual names, needs, and situations)? Would that knowledge have made your task easier or harder?
• What if you could have actually allocated resources or intangible gifts, such as time, prayer, or service? How would that have changed the exercise?

Giving God's Way

Supplies
• Bibles
• Bookzines
• Pens or pencils

(10–15 minutes)

Direct the youth to find **Deuteronomy 15:7-11** in their Bibles. Set the context for the youth (see page 64 in this book), then have one or two volunteers read the passage aloud. Refer, if necessary, to the definitions on page 61 of the bookzine. Then ask the youth to work in their teams to answer the questions on page 66 of the bookzine.

After they complete this Bible study, ask the youth whether anything would change in their allocation of funds in the previous budget activity. Allow time for group discussion.

Who Answered the Call?

Blown Away

(10–15 minutes)

Point out that celebrities, often worth millions of dollars, sometimes make headlines for large donations to specific causes, such as disaster relief, hunger relief, AIDS research. Ask the group for examples of celebrities in the news lately donating to charities or causes. Pose these rhetorical questions: What about the rest of us who don't have lots of money to give away? How do we show generosity?

Play the video vignette entitled "Who Answered the Call?" Invite the group to observe a minute of silence as they reflect upon what they saw. Then ask:

• What were your feelings as you watched this story?
• Do you have any similar stories of helping (or not)? of being helped (or not)?
• Why, do you think, is this film about generosity rather than, say, service?

A Matter of the Heart

(20–25 minutes)

Ask the youth to use their Bibles to complete the Scripture chart on page 63 of the bookzine. You may wish to assign half of the group to do half of the Scriptures (or a third of the group to a third of the Scriptures) to use time efficiently. Then have the small groups report and discuss their answers in the large group. Ask:

• What did you learn about being generous while you researched these Scriptures?

Divide the youth into pairs, and ask them to talk with each other about what they would do in each of the scenarios in "A Matter of the Heart" (bookzine, pages 64–65). After a few minutes, invite the youth to talk about their answers to the scenarios and questions they discussed with their partners. Then ask:

• What, do you think, does it mean to have a spirit of generosity and a giving heart? How does that spirit influence all of life's situations?
• Why, do you think, does God want us to be generous?

Remind the youth that, while we often think of generosity occurring in connection with how willingly a person gives away his or her money, generosity can be applied to any blessing God has given us. Generosity is a state of the heart and a matter of attitude. Challenge the youth to look for needs that they can meet generously.

Supplies
• Bibles
• *Veracity Video Vignettes, Volume 3,* ("Who Answered the Call?")
• DVD player and TV
• Bookzines
• Pens or pencils
• Dictionaries (optional)

Supplies
• Bibles
• Bookzines
• Pens or pencils

Fruitful

You cannot produce fruit by trying. Staying connected to Jesus is the only way God can bring about all that you are called to do and be.

Scripture

John 15:1-5 (Apart from me you cannot produce fruit.)

 *Additional Background*

Few of us know much about producing fruit these days. When Jesus spoke these words, the people, even the "city folk," were much closer to the source of their food. They knew about vines, branches, and caring for them. They were familiar with planting, pruning, cleaning, and removing dead branches. They were even aware of the concept of grafting new branches onto a vine.

A vine will continue to send nutrients, water, and energy to all its branches, even those that are not producing fruit. Gardeners learned to cut off the branches that were not fruitful. They also learned that more fruit is produced if you cut back the branches so that the vine can send more nutrients and water to the fruit that it is bearing.

Jesus' words didn't just connect with the people's knowledge of farming but also with their history. Several Old Testament passages refer to the image of a vine. In fact, the *Seder* or Passover meal, at which these words were likely spoken, uses "the fruit of the vine" or wine to symbolize God's goodness. Jesus knew that the people would understand these words and images at many different levels.

Jesus' focus is on fruit that is a result of abiding in him.

The branch is a carrier not the originator. The vine is the source. The branch must stay connected; it can bear fruit only as a result of its continued connection. Producing fruit is an outcome, not an effort.

Scripture is clear that we are expected to bear fruit, to have an impact as a result of our lives and faith. In fact, the consequences of not being fruitful are pretty harsh: being cut off (verse 2) and being thrown into the fire (verse 6). We may look at the consequences of not producing and, out of fear, frantically try to do it on our own.

However, Jesus' focus is on fruit that is a result of abiding in him. The word *abide* connotes choosing a place to stay and live. Abiding isn't about an occasional visit. It's about making a home and staying intimately connected.

So what fruit are we supposed to bear? Scripture points to a variety of "fruits," including in **John 15:7, 11-12,** answered prayer, joy, and love. **Galatians 5:22-24** and **2 Peter 1:5-8** refer to fruit that describe the qualities of Christian character.

The Tending and Sending parts of these lessons can be key moments of connection for your students.

John 15:1-5 isn't just about producing fruit; it's about the importance of staying connected to Jesus. By tending to our relationship to Jesus, we are preparing ourselves to bear the fruit that will result from that connection. The Tending and Sending parts of these CLAIM THE LIFE lessons can be key moments of connection for your students. In these rituals designed specifically for spiritual formation and soul tending, youth are invited to pay attention to their lives and relationship with Jesus. These weekly opportunities are great ways to reinforce for your students the importance of staying connected to Jesus every day.

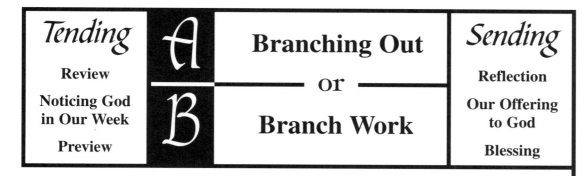

Tending	A	Branching Out	Sending
Review Noticing God in Our Week Preview	B	— or — Branch Work	Reflection Our Offering to God Blessing

Tending

(10–20 minutes) **Supplies:** *large, white candle; candleholder; matches*

❑ As the youth arrive, welcome them.

❑ Light the candle and invite the youth into this sacred space and time. Begin the "Tending to God and One Another" conversation:
- • Where were they aware of God in their week or in the world?
- • What "highs" (good things) and what "lows" (rough things) did they experience in the week?
- • What prayer requests do they have—either for themselves or on behalf of someone else?

❑ Ask the youth about their SMART goal. If they tried to live out their "offering to God" last week, how did it go? Encourage them in their discipleship efforts.

❑ Offer a prayer of thanksgiving for God's presence in the week and in the class. Lift up the group's highs and lows and prayer requests. Pray for God's guidance in this time together and along the journey.

❑ Take a few minutes to recall the previous week's word (*generosity*) and lesson. Invite those who were present to contribute to the review. Transition to the lesson (next page) by referring to today's word: *fruitful*.

Sending

(5–10 minutes) **Supplies:** *paper or notecards, pens or pencils*

❑ Ask the students to think about what it might look like if their life were bearing fruit. How would it be different? If we are called to bear fruit and the only way to do so is to stay connected to Jesus, what can they do to keep that connection healthy? Give them a few minutes to write or just think about these questions then invite a few students to offer their reflections.

❑ As the youth are ready, have them write a SMART goal (**S**pecific, **M**easurable, **A**chievable, **R**evealed, and **T**ime limited). Remind them that living SMART is their offering to God for the coming week. They may choose to frame the SMART goal around the question, "What are you going to do this week to stay connected to Jesus?"

❑ Send the group forth with a blessing of your choice or this one:

> May you recognize Jesus as the source of all good in your life. May you stay connected to that source so that your life bears good fruit in everything you do. Go in peace.

Midweek Checklist

❑ Connect with youth.
❑ Inform parents.
❑ Look over supplies and preparation for both options.

Sample SMART Goal

This week (*time limited*) **I am going to take ten minutes each morning to pray before I start my day** (*measurable*) **so that I stay better connected to Jesus and my life will bear fruit for him** (*specific, achievable, and, we trust, revealed to the individua*l)**.**

Branching Out

Staying Connected

Supplies and Preparation
- Paper
- Pens or pencils
- Large space like a parking lot, a grass field, or a gym.
- One cup per group
- One pitcher of water per group
- Some rope or space marker to define the "vine" (home base)
- A tape measure or long length of rope to measure distances
- Resources that will help the "vines" extend their reach (see the activity)
- Base the size of the teams on the available space and, of course, on the size of your group. If possible, have no fewer than 5 team members but no more than 18.

Optional Activity

Supplies
- Bookzines

(20–25 minutes)

Establish a "vine" (home base). Divide the youth into teams and give the following instructions:

The teams' goal is to create a "branch" that reaches as far as possible while always staying physically connected to the "vine." Once the branches (teams) reach as far as they think possible, they must place a cup at that spot. Then they are to take the pitcher of water from the vine, pass it along the "branch" and fill the cup. If anyone becomes disconnected from the group, and therefore the vine, the whole group must return to the base and start over.

Let the youth discover what "connected" means. They may use anything they have to stay connected (belts, jackets, shoe strings, and so on). Place resources out on the field that they can use to extend their reach (broom stick, short rope, tree branches, and so on). Challenge them to reach an area that seems impossible but is possible if they discover the resources and use them. If time allows, let them try this activity more than once to see if they can reach farther.

Once each group has placed and filled its cup, hand out paper and pens or pencils and give them two to three minutes to reflect on this activity. Ask them to consider:

- What was challenging about this activity?
- What worked and what didn't?
- What did it mean to stay connected?
- Why was staying connected important?

After a few minutes invite volunteers to talk about their thoughts. Follow up with questions that allow you to emphasize the importance of staying connected to the vine and the source of the water.

I Am the Vine

(10–15 minutes)

Refer the group to **John 15:1-5,** which is printed on page 70 of the bookzine. Read it to them and then have them read it out loud together. Ask:

- What might the cup represent?
- What might the water represent?
- According to this Scripture, who is the vine?
- What is the source of the fruit?
- What is the difference between "the source of the fruit" and "bearing fruit"?
- What does it mean to "bear fruit" in our lives? What behaviors and attitudes ("fruit") would show that a person is connected to Jesus? What would not?
- How can staying connected to one another help us? (Refer to the first activity.)
- What are some ways that we can remain connected to Jesus so that we can bear fruit?

Branch Work

Bearing Fruit

(20–25 minutes)

Direct the youth to "Two Branches" (bookzine, page 71). Hold up both branches and ask the students to write in the first section what they notice about each branch, the differences between the two, which they think will hold more fruit, and why. Tell them to just write and not tell anyone what they think yet.

Next, using the thin branch, hold it or tape the first five inches to a stable surface (table or podium) so that most of the branch hangs over the edge. Place the handles of the bag on the very end of the branch so that it is hanging in the air supported only by the branch. At this point ask the group how much "fruit" (apples, books, rocks) they think this branch will hold. Let them shout out their responses and then begin loading the fruit into the bag. Keep loading until the branch breaks. (If using a natural branch be sure that it is dry and brittle so that it snaps rather then bends. If using a dowel, you may need to tape the handles of the bag to the wood so that it doesn't slide off) Repeat this process for the thicker branch. (You can also turn the demonstration into a challenge activity by providing a set of "fruit" and branches to two or more teams.)

Once both branches have been tested, ask the students to write in the second section what they noticed. Give them about three minutes to reflect.

Ask all the students who predicted that the larger branch would hold more fruit to raise their hands. (The majority if not all the students should do so.) Ask them why they predicted the way they did. If everyone made the same prediction, you may even want to talk about why it was so obvious. Many of the answers will focus on the relative size and strength of the branch. If you use the natural branches, you may want to highlight the "freshness" of the branch as well. Ask them what they think will happen to these branches now that they aren't connected to their tree.

Strengthening the Connection

(15–20 minutes)

Refer the youth to **John 15:1-5,** printed on page 70 of the bookzine. Once everyone has it, ask them read it aloud together. Ask:

• What is the job or purpose of the branches?
• Where does the fruit come from?
• What happens if the branch isn't connected to the vine?
• If the only way for us to bear fruit is to abide in Jesus, what are some ways we can do that? What can we do to keep connected and grow stronger in our connection?

This discussion is a great opportunity to emphasize the importance of the spiritual disciplines, including coming to Sunday school and other practices of the faith. Direct the youth to "Branch Tending" (bookzine, pages 72–73). Following through on such commitments will help deepen the connection to Jesus.

Supplies and Preparation
• Bookzines
• Pens or pencils
• Two different sized branches—one long, dry branch (no more than 1/4 inch in diameter) and a newly cut healthy branch (no less than 1 inch in diameter) each about 4 feet long if possible
• "Fruit"—Use books, rocks, or other materials as weights. If you use real fruit, the youth may snack on it later; but don't let it go to waste.
• Two shopping or grocery bags (with handles) or some other way to hang the fruit from the branches
• Heavy-gauge tape, such as duct tape

Supplies
• Bookzines
• Pens or pencils

Humility

Be humble. Let go of the importance and status you think you deserve so you can really serve and love people.

Luke 14:7-11 (In humility choose the lowest place.)

Additional Background

If you choose to assume that you are important, you will likely be brought down.

Knowing that our worth is measured—not by the standards of the world but by God's love and acceptance of us—we can set aside any need for recognition from others.

Luke 14:7-11 takes place as Jesus is invited to have the Sabbath dinner at the house of an important Pharisee. Other Pharisees and prominent people in the community were also invited. This dinner was probably also a "symposia" (where we get our word *symposium*), more of a banquet or formal affair for these community leaders to check out Jesus and his teaching. These experts in the Law took this opportunity to watch Jesus very carefully to see whether he would misspeak so that they could denounce him. Having dinner or "breaking bread," especially during the Sabbath meal, meant something special in that culture. It was to be a time of good intentions, conversation, and good will. For these leaders to be looking to "trip up" Jesus did not follow the traditions of the community they were supposed to be leading.

At banquets like this one, where persons sat revealed their social status in the community. For example, on a three-person couch, the middle seat held the most honor. If the guests were sitting around a table, the person at the host's right hand was most honored and the person on the left was only slightly less honored.

In **Luke 14:7** Jesus noticed these important men all scrambling for the best seats at the table. As they were claiming the prime locations, Jesus began to tell a story about choosing seats at a banquet. This parable would not only be connected to the current situation but, for these experts in the Law, it would also recall lessons from **Proverbs 25:6-7** and other portions of the Scriptures (**Isaiah 2:12; Ezekiel 17:24; 21:26**). He encouraged them not to take the best seat and, in doing this, claim the highest honor. In fact, he said that the best move is to take the lowest seat, the worst seat in the house.

Jesus gave two good reasons to practice humility. One is practical; the other, spiritual. Practically speaking, if you take the best seat, you run the risk of being embarrassed for your actual status. If someone more important than you shows up, you not only lose your seat but might end up in the lowest of seats. If you take the bad seat and you "deserve better," the host will not let you stay there. Everyone will know how important you are when the host guides you to a better place in the room. If you choose to assume that you are important, you will likely be brought down and embarrassed. If you are humble, others will lift you up.

Jesus also gave a spiritual perspective on the importance of humility. He reminded them of God's perspective. God promised to lift up those who are down and to put down those who are up high; the proud will be humbled, while the humble will be exalted.

Humility isn't hating oneself or having a poor self-image. God gave God's own Son for us. We are valuable. Knowing that our worth is measured—not by the standards of the world but by God's love and acceptance of us—we can set aside any need for recognition from others and humbly love and serve others as followers of Christ.

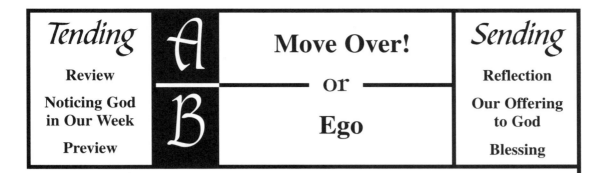

Tending	A B	Move Over! or Ego	Sending
Review Noticing God in Our Week Preview			Reflection Our Offering to God Blessing

Tending

(10–20 minutes) **Supplies:** *large, white candle; candleholder; matches*

❑ As the youth arrive, welcome them. Light the candle, and invite the youth into this sacred space and time. Begin the "Tending to God and One Another" conversation:
- Where were they aware of God in their week or in the world?
- What "highs" (good things) and what "lows" (rough things) did they experience during the week?
- What prayer requests do they have—either for themselves or on behalf of someone else?

❑ Ask the youth about their SMART goal. If they tried to live out their "offering to God" last week, how did it go? Encourage them in their discipleship efforts.

❑ Offer a prayer of thanksgiving for God's presence in the week and in the class. Lift up the group's highs and lows and prayer requests. Pray for God's guidance in this time together and along the journey.

❑ Take a few minutes to recall the previous week's word (*fruitful*) and lesson. Invite those who were present to contribute to the review. Transition to the lesson (next page) by referring to today's word: *humility*.

Sending

(5–10 minutes) **Supplies:** *paper or notecards, pens or pencils*

❑ Invite the students to spend a few minutes thinking about humility. What does it mean in the different situations of their lives to be humble? Ask them to consider how these realizations might challenge them to live differently. Give a few minutes to write or just think; then invite volunteers to share their ideas.

❑ As the youth are ready, have them write a SMART goal (**S**pecific, **M**easurable, **A**chievable, **R**evealed, and **T**ime limited). Remind them that living SMART is their offering to God for the coming week. Encourage them to consider the question "How will you set aside your ego and self-importance and live as a humble servant this week?"

❑ Send the group out with this blessing or one of your choice:

> You don't need to prove your worth to anyone—because Christ died for you. May you set aside any pride so that you can show others how much Jesus loves them too. Remember, in God's kingdom, those who try to be the greatest will be humbled; but those who live with humility will be lifted up. Go in peace.

Midweek Checklist

❑ Connect with youth.
❑ Inform parents.
❑ Look over the supplies and preparation for Option A; or have on hand *Veracity Video Vignettes, Volume 3,* for Option B.

Sample SMART Goal

I don't need to brag about myself. This week (*time limited*)**. I am going to lift others up** (*specific*) **by giving three people each day a sincere compliment** (*measurable, achievable, and, we trust, revealed to the individua*l)**.**

Move Over!

Musical Chair of Honor

Supplies and Preparation
- Bookzines
- Pens or pencils
- Chairs, especially two special ones (see the description in the activity)
- Recorded music and player
- Arrange the chairs as you would for musical chairs, only have enough chairs for everyone.

(20–25 minutes)

Along with the usual chairs, for this activity you will need two special seats. The first one is "The Seat of Honor," which can be a regular chair that you put a sign on or a special "comfy" chair. The second special seat is "The Seat of Humiliation," which can be a regular chair with a sign on it or a tiny chair borrowed from the preschool classroom.

Ask one youth not to play but to help you judge. Stress to the group that you are the host of this activity—the one who decides all disputes and whose ruling is final. This game is like musical chairs, except that there are enough seats for everyone. The challenge is to get into the seat of honor and not have to sit in the seat of humiliation.

After each round of play discuss the outcome with your helper before making your final ruling. Make a grand announcement each time of who ended up in the seat of honor. If you want to add a little spice, you can say that the person who is in the seat of honor in the very last round of play will get a prize. Play several rounds and let the youth get into it and have a fun time. Notice how many times people who are trying for the seat of honor get edged out and end up in the seat of humiliation.

End this activity with one last round. When the music stops and everyone settles into the seats, announce that this was the last round and as the host you get to declare once again who is in the seat of honor. This last time, however, tell whoever ended up in the seat of honor that he or she must get up. Tell your helper to sit in the seat of honor, since she or he deserves it for giving service to the group.

Direct the students to "Move Over!" (bookzine, page 75). Give them several minutes to respond to the questions. Invite volunteers to tell their thoughts.

The Last Shall Be First

Supplies
- Bibles
- Bookzines
- Pens or pencils

(10–15 minutes)

Have volunteers read aloud **Luke 14:7-11** and **Luke 14:1,** while the other youth follow along on page 74 of the bookzine. Ask the youth what connection the verse has to the game of musical chairs they just played. Spend several minutes talking about the connections.

Discuss several of the following questions. Guide the discussion around the idea that humility isn't about claiming and wrestling for our rights but about setting aside these rights so that we build others up and show them the love that Jesus has for them.

- In what situations in your life have you seen people try to take the best place or thing for themselves? Why do people do this?
- When we humble ourselves, does it mean that we devalue ourselves or that we think that we are worthless? (*If we are worthless, why would the host come and ask us to move up?*)
- Why, do you think, does Jesus say that we humble ourselves?

End the discussion by having a volunteer read aloud **Philippians 2:5-11.**

Ego

Simone

(15–20 minutes)

Before starting the video, ask the youth what they think humility or being humble is. Have several give their perspectives. Ask the youth to suggest some words or phrases that would be the opposite of humility. Then show the video.

When the video ends, have the group retell the story. Have five youth each tell a portion: the introduction, dancing, basketball, the girls, the end. As the main person is speaking, others may add details if needed. Encourage group story recall and commentary.

Play the video again to see how well they did putting it all together. Then ask:

- What did you notice this time that you hadn't before? What new ideas or insight came as you saw the story a second time?
- What, supposedly, is Simone's secret to success? (*The obvious response is the drink Ego.*)
- What, do you think, Ego really is? What does it represent in real life?
- What kinds of things do people rely on to build up their egos? (*For example, actions such as putting someone down or having someone they can push around, having "attitude," flashing money or muscles or good looks*)
- What does Simone think of himself and his skills? How do others perceive Simon (his real name)?

What About Chuck?

(10–15 minutes)

Turn the group's attention to Chuck. Ask:

- How would you describe Chuck? Include both negative and positive things you observed. (*He seemed lost in Simone's shadow, with no personality of his own; he didn't draw attention to himself; he was competent with the basketball; he had a taste of Ego and got rid of it.*)
- What kinds of actions and attitudes demonstrate Christian humility?
- For Christians, where does our self-worth come from? (*We know that God loves us; we don't have to show off to get attention and love from others.*)
- For Christians, where does our humility come from? (*We know that God loves all of us; all of us are special in God's eyes; all persons are of worth; our gifts and talents come from God; our gifts and talents are to be used to build up others—not just to build up ourselves.*)

Refer the youth to **Luke 14:7-11** and **Luke 14:1,** on page 74 in the bookzine. Have a volunteer read the verses aloud. Ask the youth to read the verses again to themselves and then to write on page 76 of the bookzine their responses to the questions in "What Would Jesus Say?" If you have time, invite volunteers to offer their thoughts.

Supplies
- Bibles
- *Veracity Video Vignettes, Volume 3,* ("Ego")
- DVD player and TV
- Bookzines
- Pens or pencils

 *Optional Activity*

Supplies
- Bookzines
- Pens or pencils

Light

The light of Christ can be seen in us through our words and actions.

Matthew 5:14-16 (You are to show the light to the world.)

 *Additional Background*

Light is a very big deal. The very first thing recorded in the Bible that God did was to make light. "Then God said, 'Let there be light'; and there was light' " (**Genesis 1:3**). Physically, light makes it possible for us to see what we're doing and where we're going. Spiritually, the light of Christ shows us what we should be doing and where we should be going.

God's light is given to us in the person of Jesus Christ. "For it is the God who said, 'Let light shine out of darkness,' who has shone in our hearts to give the light of the knowledge of the glory of God in the face of Jesus Christ" (**2 Corinthians 4:6**). **Ephesians 5:8-9** goes the next step: "For once you were darkness, but now in the Lord you are light. Live as children of light—for the fruit of the light is found in all that is good and right and true."

We want youth to claim light as a foundation in their faith. When persons choose to live as Jesus taught, they see and experience life in new ways. They move from darkness (lack of knowledge, blindness to the Word of God, evil, despair) to light, which brings clarity, wisdom, and hope to carry them for their whole lifetime.

> *In receiving the light of Christ, we are called to be light ourselves.*

Being "the light of the world" sounds so simple: Choose Christ, choose life, know how and live as God desires us to live. But then we are not simple. One fact of human nature is that we have free will. We have the freedom to make mistakes; to make poor decisions; to turn away from the light; to let our sinful nature take hold through our weakness, our blindness, or our rebellion. Here is where our real work begins with youth. One of our primary tasks is to help them understand the value, and God's deepest desire, of living in the light of Christ and also of being light to others.

During this year of CLAIM THE LIFE, your youth have focused on the journey of faith, learning more about what it means to claim the name and life of a Christian. Light is an appropriate way to end this year's study. In receiving the light of Christ, we are called to be light ourselves.

As we shine forth with the love of God, we bring light to the dark for others. The light is not to shine *on* us but *through* us. We began this semester with the word *glorify*. Indeed, we end with the same message: Our light—our good works—are to give glory to God, to show others the love that is God.

> *Like a city on a hill, the church too is to be a beacon and a source of light in a dark world.*

Youth also need to be reminded that Jesus' words are not just to them as individuals but also to them as a "city set on a hill." Like a city on a hill, the church too is to be a beacon and a source of light in a dark world. Together, we burn even more brightly.

Tending	A/B	No Longer Stuck	Sending
Review Noticing God in Our Week Preview		— or — **Let Your Light Shine**	Reflection Our Offering to God Blessing

Tending

(10–20 minutes) **Supplies:** *large, white candle; candleholder; matches*

☐ As the youth arrive, welcome them. Light the candle, and invite the youth into this sacred space and time. Begin the "Tending to God and One Another" conversation:
- Where were they aware of God in their week or in the world?
- What "highs" (good things) and what "lows" (rough things) did they experience during the week?
- What prayer requests do they have—either for themselves or on behalf of someone else?

☐ Ask the youth about their SMART goal. If they tried to live out their "offering to God" last week, how did it go? Encourage them in their discipleship efforts.

☐ Offer a prayer of thanksgiving for God's presence in the week and in the class. Lift up the group's highs and lows and prayer requests. Pray for God's guidance in this time together and along the journey.

☐ Take a few minutes to recall the previous week's word *(humility)* and lesson. Invite those who were present to contribute to the review. Transition to the lesson (next page) by referring to today's word: *light*.

Sending

(5–10 minutes) **Supplies:** *paper or notecards, pens or pencils*

☐ Allow time for the youth to reflect silently on the lesson. What did they discover about light as a symbol? What has become clear to them? What important things were they reminded of? What new things did they realize? Invite volunteers to share their thoughts.

☐ As the youth are ready, have them write a SMART goal (**S**pecific, **M**easurable, **A**chievable, **R**evealed, and **T**ime limited). Remind them that living SMART is their offering to God.

☐ Send the group forth with this blessing based on **Matthew 5:16** or another one of your choosing:

> God sent Jesus Christ to light our paths. Through Christ's example, may you "let your light shine before others, so that they may see your good works and give glory to [God]." Go in peace—and shine brightly!

Midweek Checklist

☐ Connect with youth.
☐ Inform parents.
☐ Look over supplies and preparation for both options.

Sample SMART Goal

This week *(time limited)* **I will light a candle every night** *(measurable)* **as a reminder to be a "light" to others around me** *(specific, achievable, and, we trust, revealed to the individual)*.

No Longer Stuck

In the Dark

(10–15 minutes)

Supplies
- Piece of black construction paper for each person (A half or a quarter of a sheet for each student is fine.)
- Markerboard or large sheets of paper
- Markers
- Bookzines
- Pens or pencils

Distribute a piece of black paper to each person. Ask these questions and list their responses on a large sheet of paper or markerboard:

- What might this black paper represent? (*darkness, night*)
- Generally, what kinds of actions do we associate with darkness or night as a symbol? (*Doing things that one wouldn't likely do when others can see what's happening, such as crime; things that cause fear; evil: "the dark side of the Force"*)
- How might persons experience darkness emotionally? (*loss, loneliness, depression, not knowing what to do to make things better, feeling helpless, feeling disappointment*)
- How do people experience spiritual darkness? (*no sense of being able to turn to God for love, comfort, or guidance; not having the support of a loving community or family; being caught up in evil, including addictions*)

Direct the youth to "Living in Darkness" (bookzine, page 78). Give them a few moments to write about experiences of darkness they have known. Assure them this writing is only for them.

Just Add Light

(20–25 minutes)

Supplies
- Bookzines
- Pens or pencils
- Glitter or metallic gel pens, white or yellow pieces of chalk, or white or light-colored crayons

Remind the group that as Christians, we have the Light—Jesus Christ—to overcome the darkness. (Refer to **John 12:46** at the bottom of page 78.) Have pairs or trios look at the list created earlier and talk about how following the Christ-light helps them and others through darkness. Give the youth two minutes, and then invite them to tell their thoughts and examples to the whole group. Affirm their contributions.

Invite a volunteer to read aloud today's Scripture (**Matthew 5:14-16**), while the other youth follow along on page 77 of the bookzine. Ask the group what they think Jesus is teaching in this passage. Have them put the message into their own words; write it out for all to see.

Give the group the pens, chalk, or crayons. Invite the youth to add light to their dark paper by drawing an illustration, symbol, or words that represent light overcoming darkness or ways that they can shine the Christ-light for others. For ideas, have them refer to today's Scripture; you may also choose to read them some "light" quotations from *www.claimthelife.com*.

Invite volunteers to tell about what they have put on their paper and why they chose what they chose. Post the creations in the room if possible.

Remind the youth that shining light for others is very difficult if you are in darkness yourself. However, Christ is there so that we don't have to remain in darkness. Encourage the youth to give over to God in prayer any darkness they feel in their lives.

Let Your Light Shine

Be the Light!

(10–15 minutes)

Recruit one responsible youth to be the "spotlight." Give him or her the large bright flashlight and instruct him or her to shine it on the youth, each in turn, as he or she is speaking (but not directly in the eyes).

Ask for a volunteer to begin this activity. Explain the following to the group:

"Raise your hand when you are ready for your turn. The spotlight will shine on you. Then you'll say: 'I am someone who (blank).' Fill in the blank with a brief, positive description of yourself."

The descriptions may be things like, "loves to sing," "is an artist," "enjoys hanging out with friends," and so forth. Use yourself as an example to show the youth how it works.

When each person who is willing has had a turn, ask:

• Usually, when the spotlight is turned on someone or something, what does it mean? (*The spotlight draws attention to the thing or person that it points at.*)

Direct the youth to today's Bible passage, **Matthew 5:14-16,** printed on page 77 of the bookzine. Have a volunteer read it aloud. Then ask:

• How is what Jesus is saying different from what we just experienced with the light? (*Our instruction from Jesus is to do good things that point to God, rather than to ourselves. Our words and actions should shine light on how things should be in the world. We are to help others see the light of Christ; it should be shining in us so brightly that others will want to find out what they're missing. We need to* be *the light.*)

Bright Ideas

(15–20 minutes)

Discuss the following questions:

• Why, do you think, do Christian youth sometimes hide their light? (*fear of rejection, fear of being different*)
• What are some ways that you as an individual can let your light shine so that others will see God? (*through good works*)
• How is the church like a "city on hill"? What are some ways the church can shine light in the world? Give some examples.
• How does being part of the church help us shine light for others?
• Do you want people to know who did the good deed for them or who provided what they needed? Why, or why not? Think both about yourself as an individual and about the church as you discuss this question.
• Why is it important, sometimes, that persons in need *do* know who helped them? Give an example.
• When Christians help others, on whom should the spotlight shine? (*God*)

Supplies
• One large, bright flashlight
• Bookzines

Optional Activities

A Bonus: Ebenezer

Take Away Raising our Ebenezer is a statement of faith: God has been with us thus far; we trust that God will continue to be with us.

Scripture **1 Samuel 7:12** (God is with us thus far.)

Tending

Begin with your Tending ritual as usual. After tending to God and one another, tell the youth that today's word is *Ebenezer*. Undoubtedly, it will produce some interesting responses, since the word is rarely used today, except in reference to Ebenezer Scrooge in the Charles Dickens's story *A Christmas Carol*.

Teaching

Supplies and Preparation
- Bibles
- Hymnals
- Bookzines
- Pens or pencils
- 16 sheets of paper
- Marker
- Enough stones for every youth to have one (Small, smooth ones will be best so that the youth can carry them with them all of the time.)
- Write out this semester's 16 words each on one piece of paper. Lay them at random on the floor in the room.

Optional Activities

Have a volunteer read aloud **1 Samuel 7:12.** Give this background:

> The people of God, like us, were on a faith journey. Sometimes they wandered away from God; sometimes they deliberately turned away from God to worship other gods. But despite their sin and disloyalty, God was always with them, working in their lives, inviting them back into a fuller and better relationship. Through a series of events, the people realized how important God was to them and renewed their covenant to serve only the Lord. At this point in the Scripture, they once again had seen proof of God's love for them. Samuel erected the stone as a reminder that God had been with them. Raising the Ebenezer stone is also a statement of faith: God has been with us thus far; God will *continue* to be with us.

Invite the youth to think about their own journeys of faith, especially during this semester. Have the youth silently "journey" from their place to two or more of the words that represent something meaningful for them in their faith. At the particular words, they may simply write their names on the paper or they may also add a note.

After a few minutes, encourage volunteers to talk about their "ebenezer words." What has been particularly meaningful for them? Why?

Refer the youth to verse 2 of the hymn "Come, Thou Fount of Every Blessing" (check your hymnal). Point out that in looking back at what God has done in their lives and looking forward in faith, they too are raising their Ebenezer.

Give each youth a stone as an Ebenezer, a reminder that God is with us and that God will continue to be.

Sending

Encourage the youth to write a SMART goal. Send them forth with this blessing:

> God is with us. God is with us indeed! Let us continue the journey with that assurance. Go in peace.